Success
2000

Success 2000

Moving into the Millennium with Purpose, Power, and Prosperity

Vicki Spina

John Wiley & Sons, Inc.

New York ▲ Chichester ▲ Weinheim ▲ Brisbane ▲ Singapore ▲ Toronto

Copyright © 1997 by Vicki Spina
Published by John Wiley & Sons, Inc.

Library of Congress Cataloging-in-Publication Data:

Spina, Vicki.
   Success 2000 : moving into the millennium with purpose,
power, and prosperity / by Vicki Spina.
     p. cm.
   Includes bibliographical references.
   ISBN 0-471-17184-0 (pbk. : alk. paper)
    1. Vocational guidance. 2. Career development.
  3. Success. I. Title.
  HF5381.S7353 1997
  650.1—dc21   96-46711

To those individuals who thirst for knowledge
and yearn to enjoy the journey
and fully participate in the school of life.

Acknowledgments

To my mom, Nancy Johnson. Your courage inspired me to grow beyond my beliefs. Your love has always given me comfort, even now your love lives in my heart and soul.

To Anita Brick. My dear friend, mentor, and advisor. You inspire me beyond words! (And you know I'm seldom speechless!) I know I can always count on you. Thanks, Brickie, for being "you."

To Deborah Hawkins. You came into my life at the perfect time! You're not only a talented writer, this book wouldn't have been completed without your help. Thank you.

To Wendy Kellerman. Your tenacity, unfailing belief in me, and friendship made this book a reality.

To Mike Hamilton. Thanks for taking a risk on this book.

To Kathleen O'Regan. You are the most insightful woman I know. All your visions for me are coming to fruition. Thank you for sharing your gifts and friendship with me. Together we are "Warriors of Light." I love you.

To Gary Baylor. Without your financial support, my dreams would be just that—dreams. Thank you for helping out a struggling entrepreneur.

To James Savage. Thank you for teaching me forgiveness.

To Nancy Juckett. My angel friend.

To my sweet and loving daughters, Carli and Caitlyn. Thank you for making me laugh, helping me to see life through your eyes, and for being the best kids a mom ever dreamed of. You two are the epitome of "Success." I love you with every breath I take.

These acknowledgments would not be complete without giving *full credit and everlasting love to my life's partner, true father, and creator*—God.

Contents

If I can stop one heart from breaking,
I shall not live in vain;
If I can ease one life the aching,
Or cool one pain,
Or help one fainting robin
Unto his nest again,
I shall not live in vain.

Emily Dickinson

Define troublesome feelings:

① after a few yrs in RES NYC, MIA,
JFK FTO, work hard and find the
only compensation would be to get a
promotion that wasn't very appealing,
(i.e. longer hours w/o being compensated
appropriately, working strange hours)
~~many~~ promotions

Introduction

Success is not having what you want, but wanting what you have.
Anonymous

How would it feel to know that right now in your life, you are exactly where you are meant to be? **YOU ARE!** You might say, "Then why do I need this book?" You don't! (Are you tempted to put this book back? Before you do, read a few more paragraphs.) You **need** water, food, and sleep; *you don't* **need** *fixing.* You are not "broken," in need of repair. You might *desire* to have a better life; you wouldn't have picked up this book in the first place if you didn't desire more out of life. **Success 2000 is designed to help you achieve your desires.**

Would you be comforted to know that in the whole scheme of things in life, you are at the "right" place? Or would you feel sad or angry about your circumstances? Whether you are comforted by this knowledge or it brings up less-than-joyful feelings, you will learn—through this book and the massive changes our society is currently going through—that you ARE exactly where you are meant to be right now and that **you are ready for the next step.** This is why you've purchased this book. You are ready and the time is now!

Looking back over the past few years, I realize how resistant I was to believing that my life was moving along perfectly and I was indeed exactly at the right place. I fought hard to disprove this theory. I was convinced I was supposed to be further along than I was and I would not be happy or content until I got there. It took several years and the same mistakes time and again before I decided to assume a different view. Once I accepted this new way of looking at things, my career and ultimate success in business blossomed. *Success 2000* is the guide I followed, and you can too!

You are now preparing to enter the twenty-first century. That sounds like a ride from Tomorrowland at Disney World, doesn't it? Have we finally begun the descent into the millennium? Yes for some, no for others. It all depends on you. Are you still struggling to hold onto outdated beliefs or are you excited about the journey to unknown horizons? Whatever your answer, *this book is for you!* For those with a healthy sense of adventure, you'll learn how to enhance what you already know and make the transition more enjoyable. For those who are a bit more skeptical and resistant to change (yes, you know who you are), you'll learn some new techniques and behaviors that may serve you better. *Wouldn't you like to make work and life fun again?*

For the reader who remains optimistic and open-minded, this book will move along quite fluently, enhancing your journey along the way. For the reader who prefers challenges, hurdles, obstacles, and the like, I will ask of you to lay down your sword and defenses. You won't be needing them while engaged in this book. If after reading this material, you choose to pick them up again, you are welcome to. I assure you, however, that you will look at your defenses in a totally different light. You see, I know this from experience. I certainly could have written the book entitled "Life Is a Struggle" (you probably could have as well). Instead I chose to write this book. Why?

Six years ago I was burned out, exhausted, and totally disenchanted with my career. Having spent almost 15 years as a recruiter, I was tired of the daily grind and felt helpless about where my career was going. Sundays were the worst. I'd start by looking at the want ads, although I knew even before I opened the paper that I'd not find anything in there for me. As the day progressed, I grew more upset by my thoughts of starting another Monday doing something that no longer interested me. Week after week, month after month, my days were spent "just hanging in there" until Friday.

Why was I so unhappy? I made a pretty good living. I could perform my job in my sleep. I was very good at my profession. What was happening to me? Was I having a midlife crisis at 33? Wasn't that supposed to happen at 40? As these thoughts nagged at me day after day, I began to question my own existence. Why was I here on this planet? Was this the best life would ever be? Why couldn't I be content with what I had? Was I the only one who felt this way? These questions were unrelenting. One day a coworker suggested we go to a seminar called "Understanding Yourself and Others" (produced by Global Relationship Seminars, Austin, TX). I immediately agreed. After all, I wasn't doing so well on my own, so why not see what I could learn from them?

They say that pain can be a great motivator. It took a lot of pain to get me there. When I walked into the workshop that night, the facilitators explained that they wouldn't be providing any answers that weekend. We had to do all the work ourselves. "Great," I thought to myself, "if I knew the answers, I wouldn't need to be here!" The facilitators proceeded to explain how we all build protections in this life that prevent us from getting the results we desire. In order to learn to get what we desire, we must choose to be in "a learning mode," not a "proving" one. This struck a chord with me. I was so accustomed to showing everyone how much I knew that I had difficulty revealing to anyone how much I didn't know. As the group shared some common protections, I made a commitment to myself that evening to do things differently. I decided to give 110% effort toward learning how to be happy again. Little did I know at that time how much my life would change!

A wise person once told me to "write about what I know." And so I am, in hopes of sharing the knowledge I have gained in order to make your journey a bit more enjoyable. You can choose to learn from the "school of hard knocks" and reinvent the wheel, or you can learn at my expense and avoid some painful and costly mistakes along the way. Either way you will learn. Life's lessons are not options. Only what lessons and how you learn them are. It is all up to you. Only you can make the choice.

I promise you this much (and I don't make promises lightly), *you will always be in the driver's seat—I won't tell you what to do.* I only offer a map to get to your destination via the scenic highway. At any time you can choose the back roads, traffic jams, and industrial routes. There is no right or wrong way. This book will be as easy or as difficult as you decide. Either way, from reading and studying this book (map) you will discover the following: whether you are "living" or merely "surviving"; how to assess where you are now in your career path and determine where you choose to go; how to find your special and unique purpose in life; how to create a plan outlining small, easy steps to build a bridge to your destination; how to reclaim your personal and career power to take advantage of all the changes going on and manage them instead of them managing you; how to enjoy the ride and flow easily downstream instead of fighting futilely upstream; how to develop a winning career plan to boost your current value and get the most money possible in the future; hundreds of tips and ideas on how to learn "what's going on out there" and how to use this information to your advantage; how to stay ahead of your competition by creating win-win opportunities; how to engage public relations and image-building tactics to leverage your career; and also how to determine what your options are for better educating yourself and how to implement them in your life.

In addition, you'll learn how to take the "work" out of networking and have more fun, you'll understand how "cultural diversity" affects us all and why volunteering can make your life and others' more full and rewarding, and you'll develop a prosperous mind-set to make more money. You'll find out how to spot new career trends and stay ahead of the times, how to change careers quickly and painlessly, and finally, how to balance it all!

We're going to start our journey by taking a look at how times have changed these past few years and what you can expect. So get comfortable, take a deep breath, and come along for the ride that could be the ride of your life! Because it is my intention to have this book be an interactive experience with you the reader, I will from time to time ask you to get involved in the process of discovering your own personal success. So before you begin, complete the following statement: "Success to me means _____

_____ ."

At the end of this book you will have the opportunity to again complete this statement. It will be interesting to see if your views are the same.

► *1* ◄

Adapting to a New Way of Life without Losing Your Mind

**The trouble with life in the fast lane
is that you get to the other end in an awful hurry.**
John Jensen

How many of you reading this book are just feeling "sick and tired" of being sick and tired? Actually, recognizing that you are fed up with how your life is going is not such a bad thing. Or perhaps you feel your life is average but something is lacking and it could be better? Before any change can occur, we first must choose to become aware of where we are in life.

Waking Up from the "Deep Sleep"

For years I was not aware of much in my life. I was fast asleep. Almost zombielike, in fact. I was in what you would call a "survival" mode. Oh sure, I looked awake, I was able to function in my day-to-day activities, and no one knew I was in a walking coma. (Most likely because they were in a similar coma.) This state of survival has become commonplace in today's busy world. We are so busy executing our robotlike functions that we cease to even recognize what is happening to us. So day after day, week after week, and year after year, we continue forcing

1

ourselves to get up in the morning, go to work, eat, sleep, and fulfill our human roles.

Occasionally we attempt to awaken ourselves or others. We've even attempted to jump-start ourselves with millions of gallons of Starbucks coffee each day. To no avail. We have read thousands of self-help books (only to be told we are more messed up than we thought) and listened to countless motivational speakers, gurus, and the like. You can't fault us for trying, right? Well, from this point on, I am going to suggest you *stop trying*. **NO MORE TRYING.** After all, trying is probably the biggest factor in your feeling sick and tired. Instead, I recommend you begin this book by *relaxing* and **becoming aware again.**

Have you ever watched a child who's taking a walk? How they notice everything? "Look!" they squeal with excitement, "a ladybug." Soon after, they notice something else, like how the clouds look like a big elephant or that the trees wave to them. Children are fully awake and aware of their surroundings. They haven't been conditioned to shut out the world the way the adults around them have.

I'm not sure when I "fell asleep"; it was a gradual process. However, I remember the exact moment I was jarred out of my sleep by an intense pain in my stomach (quite commonly known as an ulcer). "Wait a minute . . ." I said, "I'm only 26 years old—I'm not supposed to get an ulcer!" My doctor patiently informed me that indeed I was rather young to have such a condition; however, age was not the cause—my lifestyle was. Stress, overwork, poor nutrition, and so on were the reasons. At the time I was diagnosed with the ulcer, I was also two months' pregnant. The doctor cautioned me to slow down, and due to the possible side effects, I would not be able to take any medication. **Wake-up call number 1.**

About two years later I received wake-up call number 2—a divorce. Number 3 came when I was fired from my job. (I wish I could stop here and say that I finally woke up completely; however, I wasn't ready yet.) It took several more events (being diagnosed with chronic fatigue syndrome, becoming unemployed again, losing my home, and going bankrupt) before I was able to finally rouse myself from my stupor long enough to start becoming aware of "how my life was happening to me."

In order to help you begin the awareness process (and for most of you, I'll bet you have already begun or you wouldn't be reading this book), the following questionnaire will assist you in determining a self-evaluation of where you are right now:

Questionnaire: Are You Living or Merely Surviving?

	Yes	No	1/22 Yes No
1. If you found out today that you had only six months to live, would you be living and working where and how you are now?		X	K
2. Do you often consider yourself refreshed and energetic?		x	X
3. Are you healthy, free from recurring colds, sinus headaches, and so on?	X		X
4. Are your relationships with family, friends, bosses, and coworkers happy and fulfilling?		X	X
5. Can you remember what you like to do for fun? Do you have a favorite hobby or interest that you look forward to?	X		X
6. Do you live comfortably on your salary with money left over for "fun" things?	x		X
7. Do you know your purpose in life and are you fulfilling your potential?	X		X
8. Do you do things you enjoy every day (as opposed to only weekends and holidays)?	X		X
9. Do you feel enthusiastic and excited to get up in the morning?	X		X
10. Can you think of at least three new things that you've learned this week?	X		X
11. Do you trust your feelings (or do you constantly second-guess yourself and rely mainly on others' opinions)?		X	X
12. Do you plan "fun time" for yourself each day?			
13. Do you feel your life is full and you have no regrets?		X	X
14. Do you like yourself and seldom envy others?	X		X
15. Are you happy most of the time?	X		X

If you answered NO to more than three of the above questions, YOU ARE IN SURVIVAL MODE! Survival mode is a form of protection that we build in order to avoid pain. There aren't too many of us that actually enjoy pain. So, not having learned healthy ways to go through pain or cope with it, we instead learn to avoid it. However, what many of you have discovered (myself included) is that *avoiding pain is only a temporary fix.* Sooner or later, the actions we take to avoid the pain end up causing more of it. In order to learn how to start living again instead of just surviving, it is important to become aware of where you currently are in your life and why you are there.

Wherever You Are—BE There!

Okay, so you've awakened enough to realize that where you are is not all that great. Immediately you judge this to be bad or wrong. *In fact, just the opposite is true!* **You are exactly where you are supposed to be right now in the whole scheme of life.** Often when our lives are "going along pretty well," we develop a comfort zone and fail to grow. Adversity and challenge *may be* needed for us to move to the next level in life. As I mentioned in the introduction, you can be comforted by this knowledge or feel sad or angry about it. Fill in the following sentence: "Hypothetically, I am exactly where I am meant to be (in the exact right place) in my life right now and I feel _challenged_ ." and a little ~~and~~ frustrated

Sad   Angry   Disappointed   Relieved   Happy   Depressed

Or respond: "I don't feel anything—I don't feel bad—I always knew my life would end up this way." If this is an accurate statement, then fill in "hopeless."

Let's briefly look at these feelings. After all, **how you feel about your life will create the thoughts you have, and the thoughts you have create your reality.** Once you discover your reality (when you aren't sleeping, that is), you can then make some choices about your life, rather than your life choosing for you!

If you felt sad, angry, disappointed, depressed, or hopeless to learn you are at the right place in your life, chances are that you had a plan (or expectation) for yourself and your life, and it hasn't yet materialized. Because your life is not going according to your plan or expectation, you are probably not experiencing true peace of mind. "Success is not having what you want, but *wanting what you have.*" When you adapt this statement and philosophy to your life, you will at last feel some peace of mind.

Understanding How You Got to Where You Are (and Learning to Accept It!)

The first rule of living a life of success (and enjoying peace of mind) is to **have no specific expectations!** Yet we all have them, don't we? And our expectations aren't always positive ones. We may feel that "life is a struggle . . . and then you die." Or you may feel angry (at yourself or life) for not being where you want to be by now. Whatever feelings you are having about this topic, know that your feelings are valid. *I am not here to change how you feel.* Instead, I would like to suggest that the feelings you have are perfect tools to use for self-assessment and to discover how to have a more rewarding life and career.

For those of you who answered that you felt sad about where your life is (or disappointed, depressed, or angry), take a moment to ask yourself, "Where did I **expect** to be right now?" "Did I **expect** to be further along?" Now apply **rule number 1** in life: have no expectations. Ask yourself how you might feel if you didn't expect to be further along and *understood your life is moving along at the right pace.* How would you feel? Take a moment to reflect on these feelings.

When I first learned that I was exactly where I was meant to be in life, I was extremely angry and also very sad. I was 33 years old, divorced, bankrupt, and miserable! I truly believed that someone had played a cosmic joke on me and that my life should really be like *The Dick Van Dyke Show.* (I guess I watched too much TV growing up.) Instead of having great neighbors like Millie and Jerry, I didn't even have a home (I lost that too.) Of course hindsight is always 20/20, and I realized eventually that my life was indeed right on course. Had I not lost my job and gone through the events I went through, I would not have had the insight, empathy, and knowledge to assist others in their career endeavors. If I had accepted my life during the turbulent times, I would have had a much more enjoyable time. Instead, I fought it with vengeance and proceeded to try harder—only to end up back where I started . . . unhappy and frustrated.

In order to truly believe you are exactly where you are meant to be, you must first have a faith or belief system that you have more of a purpose in life than just taking up space on the planet. Without this faith, life makes very little sense. So, how do you get this kind of faith if you don't have it?

All we require in order to get this faith is to choose it. Then, be open to receiving it in whatever way is for your best and highest good. Sounds simple, doesn't it? It can be. However, many of us believe that in order to have great faith or sense of purpose, it must be a difficult process. It may indeed take something major to shake you up a bit and awaken you to this knowledge, or it may just take you giving yourself permission to have it. One of the main reasons I decided to write this book was to help you become aware you can do things differently without necessarily having to endure a great deal of pain or hardship. Rather, you can learn from me and others instead of the school of hard knocks. (Unless, of course, you are like me and are meant to learn it this way for your highest good.)

Take a look once again at what you have expected from life. *Write down your expectations.* Next, replace all your expectations with the following statements: "I am open to my life working according to my best and highest good. I will not judge the events in my life as good or bad—instead, I believe it isn't what happens to me that matters, but rather how I react to those events. I am exactly where I am meant to be in my life right now." For example, when I became aware of where I was in my life, honestly viewed my expectations (and negative judgments) about being 33 years old and out of work, and replaced these beliefs with "I am open to my life working according to my best and highest good," I was able to stop kicking myself for being a failure and begin the process of learning to feel good about myself again.

Learning to Feel Okay Again

I sincerely believe we spend the first 20 years or so of our lives learning "how to live life" and the rest of our lives learning to "undo" what we've learned! Have you ever noticed that people who believe that they are lucky are lucky? And then there is the rest of the world, those who believe they aren't lucky—they usually aren't. (In fact, they'll often go out of their way to prove it to you!) Dr. Wayne Dyer talks about this subject in his tape series *How to Be a No-Limit Person* (Nightingale Conant, 1980). He tells a story about the person who always gets the parking space near the door. Dr. Dyer explains that those who believe they will find the space close by will look for it. He also reminds us that the people who automatically assume they won't find a space close by (because they think there never are any) won't look for a spot up close. So, if your *intentions* are not to find a parking space close by the door, what kind of *results* will you get? Whatever you intend in life—you will see those results. Let's examine how understanding the law of intentions and results will affect how you feel about yourself and life.

Intentions = Results

Understanding that your intentions equal your results is **rule number 2** of a successful life! **Intentions** are different from expectations. According to *Webster's II New Riverside Dictionary* (New York: Berkley Book, 1989), to intend is "to have a plan of action or an aim that guides action." To expect is "to look into the future with a certain belief of the outcome." Therefore, if you expect to get promoted and it doesn't occur (in the time frame or way you thought it would), you may be disappointed or angry, and this affects your peace of mind. Instead, if you place your intentions on "having peace of mind" and allowing the events in your life to flow according to your highest good, even if you don't get the promotion you'll be able to react positively instead of negatively.

To further explore the concept of "intentions = results" requires that you take a stroll down memory lane. *Think of one time in your life when you set a 100% intention on achieving a goal and you did it.* Perhaps it was attending college. Did you attend college? If you did, then ask yourself, "Was it my intention to go to college?" Yes, your intention was to go to college and the result was that you went to college. (Now, you may say although you went to college, it was really your parents' intention for you to go, not yours. Then you can ask yourself, "Was it my intention to please my parents by honoring their intention for me?") Next, ask yourself, "Did I complete college?" Yes or no. If you answered yes, wouldn't you agree that it was indeed your intention to finish college? If you answered no, wouldn't you agree that somewhere along the way you made a choice not to finish (or revised your initial intention)?

Next, while looking back at your past intentions, recall an event from which you ended up with a result you believed to be bad or wrong. (Take time to do this now.) When I was writing my first book,

Getting Hired in the '90s (Chicago: Dearborn Publishers, 1995), it was my intention to finish the book in six months. When it wasn't completed even after a year's time, I found ways to justify why it wasn't finished. (Boy, did I ever come up with a list. . . . no time, kids interfering, it was harder than I thought, etc.) I fought to the very end to convince myself and others it was my intention to finish within one year. I believed I wasn't in control of all the circumstances that prevented me from completing the book. I finally came to understand that although my original intention was to complete the book in six months, somewhere along the way I had changed my original intention. When I decided to commit to a new 100% intention of completing the book when it was for my best and highest good, I was able to enjoy the process of writing more (without all the pressure), and the book was completed shortly thereafter. (And of course it did work out perfectly. Had the book come out when I had originally expected, it probably wouldn't have sold very well. I had self-published the first edition, and bookstores rarely purchased books from small independents like me. However, with the new breed of superstore book chains cropping up in the early '90s and needing to stock 10,000 to 100,000 titles, bookstores became more flexible in working with small presses and decided to purchase directly from me. The old saying "Timing is everything in life" truly applies here.)

In order to start feeling "okay" about yourself and your life, you must *take responsibility for all of your intentions and results whether you deem them good or bad, right or wrong*. The first step in this process is setting your intentions on becoming aware of where you are currently (as I stated earlier, you can't change or improve anything you aren't aware of first). After that, you can choose to place your intent on gaining the beliefs that will help you accept that where you are in life is where you are meant to be.

Making a New Agreement with Yourself

Complete the following agreement with yourself.

I, _____, *now take charge of my life*
        (print your name)
and set my intentions on first becoming aware of my current beliefs; next,
developing new beliefs that will assist me in accepting and enjoying my life

as it is now (by learning not to judge its events as good or bad); and fi-nally, giving myself permission to allow my life to flow according to what-ever is for my best and highest good.

_____   _____

Signed   Date

TIP I suggest writing the above agreement on a three-by-five-inch card and placing it where you can look at it and remind yourself of your intentions often.

Once you've adapted this belief and truly accepted it as the truth that creates your reality, you can then assume the belief systems that support feeling good about yourself and your life up to this point. Before you can assume new beliefs that may serve you and your life more successfully, you can choose to take an inventory of what you currently believe.

Uncovering Your Beliefs

Complete the following self-assessment. At the end of the questionnaire add as many beliefs to the list as possible. Be completely honest with yourself during this assessment; you are not doing yourself any favors by judging your answers and making yourself look more optimistic than you truly are. Practice being nonjudgmental during this exercise and view your answers with the thought of "isn't that interesting I believe this way." Remember, beliefs are learned—you can *learn* new beliefs that better suit your life!

What Are My Beliefs?

	Yes	No
1. I believe my life is working perfectly.	X	___
2. I believe that I am exactly where I am meant to be right now (in the whole scheme of things).	X	___
3. I believe we can enjoy our career and that it doesn't have to be hard work.	X	___

(continued)

Beliefs (*continued*)

	Yes	No
4. I believe that I have a special purpose in life (even though I am not quite sure what it is).	X	
5. I believe my identity isn't what I "do" for a living and that I offer this world many unique and special talents.	X	
6. I believe that my thoughts create my reality.	X	
7. I believe I am currently living my life successfully.		X
8. I believe "intentions = results."	X	
9. I believe I am accountable for how I react to events in my life.	X	
10. I believe the changes going on in today's work world and society are only going to improve our world.	X	
11. I believe my life is as good or as bad as I desire it to be.	X	

Next, take out a piece of paper and write down two beliefs about yourself, two beliefs about your life, and two beliefs about your world. Example:

My Self   *My Life*   *My World*

_____   _____   _____

_____   _____   _____

Additional notes and beliefs:

_____

_____

There are no right or wrong beliefs. However, there are beliefs that you have currently that may no longer serve you in reaching your intention of having a successful life. Make a list of the beliefs that no longer serve you in your intention of "allowing your life to flow perfectly according to your highest good":

Beliefs That Are No Longer Serving Me

1. _____

2. _____

3. _____

4. _____

5. _____

6. _____

Example: "I believe that in order to be successful I must work hard." This is a common belief that many of us grew up with. It was passed down from generation to generation. According to *Webster's II New Riverside Dictionary*, the word *hard* means "difficult to perform, comprehend, or endure." If it is your intention to have difficulty with life, what do you think your results will be? (Remember, intentions = results). Replace this current belief with one that better fits your new intention. "I believe success is having what I choose and accepting it joyfully; therefore, I am successful now and happy and grateful for where I am right now." A great book to assist you in accepting and healing your current work situation is Dr. Charles Mallory's *Workhealing* (Marina del Rey, CA: DeVorss Publications, 1994).

Stretching Your Comfort Zone—Comfortably

Now that you know where you are, you can determine your current "comfort zone." Your comfort zone is made up of the beliefs, thoughts, and attitudes that you've grown accustomed to. Even if we decide to learn and adapt new beliefs to change the results we choose in life, often we find ourselves experiencing difficulty in getting past our comfort zone (see Figure 1.1).

Success consists of a series of little daily efforts.
Mamie McCullough

Often when making a decision to change ourselves, we focus on the destination first. In this case, we may focus on getting to destination Z when in between seems like the Grand Canyon. Taking a

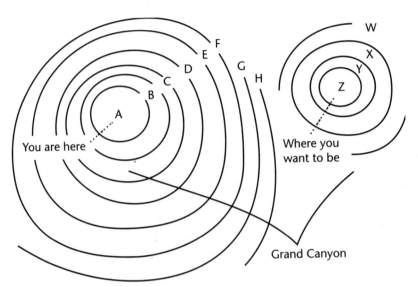

By stretching your comfort zone one step at a time,
you'll get to point Z without major discomfort.

Figure 1.1 Stretching Your Comfort Zone.

running leap off the side to reach Z appears overwhelming, dangerous, and out of our league. Yet we often attempt this, fail, and make a
new decision to just forget our dreams. "I tried and couldn't do it!"
That is exactly what happened in my life when I began writing my
first book. With little planning or forethought, I delved into the project unprepared and fell right into the canyon. Headfirst. Crash! I felt
worse about myself at that time because by then I was awake and
aware of all my possibilities—and still I wasn't achieving anything.
Ignorance can be bliss. I beat up on myself pretty good. However, I
soon learned my mistake of jumping off the side of the canyon without a safety net or a bridge. I decided to do it differently. Rather than
focus on getting to Z, I began the process of focusing on stretching my
comfort zone (just enough that I could manage) to B instead. Once I
got to B, I proceeded to C, and so on. Through these small manageable steps I was able to gently stretch my comfort zone, and I soon arrived unscathed at destination Z. In fact, I don't even recall the exact

moment I got there (it was rather anticlimactic). One day I just realized I had arrived and smiled. I then began the process again when I chose another goal.

Ten Tiny Steps to Building the Bridge from Where You Are to Where You Choose to Be!

Anita Brick, founder of The Encouragement Institute, has designed an easy and fun way to help you stretch your comfort level and achieve your goals. Six years ago Anita Brick owned a successful human resources consulting firm in Chicago. One evening when she was on her way to meet some friends, her life changed forever. Anita was exiting the elevator of her apartment building when the elevator plunged down one and a half floors. Within a few brief seconds she was pinned to the wall of the elevator shaft and nearly severed in half. It took the jaws of life to set her free. Actually, she was far from being "free." It took Anita years of physical and emotional healing and therapy to put her life back together. By understanding and putting these powerful yet manageable steps to use in her life, Anita was able not only to recover from this devastating event but also go on to write two books, teach workshops, and inspire others. *These steps are not only for individuals who have faced incredible adversity, they are for anyone who chooses to enhance one's current life and circumstances:*

Ten Tiny Steps

1. See where you are—make an honest self-evaluation.
2. Accept where you are—you are exactly where you are meant to be (wherever you are, be there).
3. Bring in an outside party (a friend or consultant) to help in this process.
4. Make a list of *appropriate* goals. Be honest with yourself. These goals will look different to different people and at different times in your life. (Example: If you are currently a couch potato, an appropriate goal may be to take a walk around the block. However, if you are a marathon runner, your goal would be different.) These goals are set to challenge you just a tiny bit.
5. Cross off all the goals on your list that *you really wouldn't do* and are inconsistent with other parts of your life. Example: If you

have dreamed about joining the Peace Corps but are not willing to live an impoverished lifestyle for several years, cross it off your list and replace it with something you *would be willing* to do.

6. Look at the remaining goals and choose one (the easiest and most enjoyable).
7. Look at the goal and **decide what part of the goal you can do right now.** Is the goal in its present form still too big? *Keep breaking it down until you can actually take action.*
8. **Take action!**
9. If you are not able to accomplish this goal, go back to step 5 and repeat the process.
10. Have fun and balance the easiest, most enjoyable goals with those you might be tempted to put off. Reward yourself when you achieve a goal.

TIPS ON USING THE TEN TINY STEPS

▶ Use a journal to write down your steps.
▶ Work in 24-hour increments.
▶ Review steps daily to check status (or periodically, depending on the goal you've set).
▶ If after reviewing your status, you see you are not taking action, go back to step 5 and plan a different appropriate step (you may just decide you are no longer interested in pursuing this goal or set a future date to pursue it). If you are taking action, continue planning the next steps to lead to a bigger challenge.
▶ Use your journal to record your weekly accomplishments. Remember, even the small steps are a big deal. Congratulate yourself for ALL accomplishments.

A journey of a thousand miles begins with a single step.
Anonymous

Earlier I spoke of the time I sabotaged myself by "jumping off the cliff" when writing my first book. By using the above tiny steps, I was able to stretch my comfort zone from A to B, and so on. We live in a society in which we celebrate overnight sensations, and once we decide on what we choose, we want it yesterday. It takes a strong foundation in order to have a sturdy structure to build on and one that will support your life successfully over the years. The Ten Tiny Steps will help you do just that. Build your confidence level to take bigger and bigger steps down the road.

Patti MacArthur was ready to "jump off the cliff" when I first met her. Distraught and emotionally burned out from her job and life, she was ready to walk into her boss's office and give two weeks' notice. Patti was a sales representative who had worked for the same firm for two years. Patti had achieved a fair amount of recognition (both financially and through awards) during her tenure with her company. But times had changed and the bottom line was issued to all employees. Either make more sales or be fired. Patti's initial reaction to this ultimatum was to quit before she was fired. She informed me that she was "too burned out" to go back out on the streets and sell harder. Patti also explained she no longer felt sales was the job for her. By utilizing the Ten Tiny steps, we were able to devise a plan and strategy that resulted in a win-win situation for all concerned.

We first identified (self-assessment) where Patti was, both emotionally and in her career. She admitted that over the past several months she had not been putting in 100% at her job. And she also was honest enough to state that she wasn't willing to give any more to her job (acceptance). Patti took step number 3 (bring in an outside party) by hiring me. We proceeded to step 4 (set appropriate goals), outlining steps that would challenge her just a tiny bit. I asked Patti how she would feel about herself if she were to quit her current job right then. Patti said that she would feel like she had failed. Rather than make her goal to look for a new job, we shifted her goal to feeling better about herself today. Patti was candid in admitting that she would feel a whole lot better if she would make one more sale before she left, just so she could "show them." I suggested instead of proving herself to others, to prove it to Patti. Patti had forgotten what a good salesperson she was. She agreed that her attitude wasn't too good, and this might affect her getting a new position. An appropriate goal for Patti was to do something that would help her feel better about herself again. I encouraged Patti to make it something fun and easy. We came up with a list of steps she could take and crossed off the things on her list that she really wouldn't do (step 5). Patti ended up with three steps she could take and then chose the most enjoyable one. She always enjoyed talking to friendly people, and there was one client in particular that she enjoyed more than most. I encouraged her to call him that day (keep breaking it down until you can take action). Patti phoned him immediately (take action). Her client was happy to hear from her and appreciated her letting him know that he was one of her favorite clients. After Patti made the call she did feel better about herself. This encouraged her to call more people. Before she knew it, she had made 10 sales calls.

One of these calls would prove to change her whole life! Patti telephoned a major client who had been on the fence about making a decision. Patti's attitude was upbeat and friendly this day (she wasn't living in fear or desperation about lack of sales or losing her job), and the client responded with enthusiasm. He made a decision to invite her in to give her presentation. Patti was so excited about getting her foot in the door she forgot all about quitting. The following week Patti closed the largest sale in her region's history. On her second visit to me she decided that although she was happy with her progress and new attitude, she still wanted to look for a new job. However, now she made the decision while she maintained "peace of mind" rather than fear. Her confidence was at an all-time high, so instead of leaving sales altogether, she chose to remain in sales and become a manager. Within three weeks, she landed a sales manager position with a competitor and raised her salary by more than $20,000 annually. Patti was able to resign her current position with dignity and left a good last impression at her company.

List, in the space provided, one step you can take today to move closer to feeling better about yourself. (Example: I will read ALL of Chapter 1 of *Success 2000* and complete the exercises. If this is still too large a goal, break it down: I will read three pages per day, or something to that effect.)

My tiny step today is _____.

How many times have you *reacted* to life and problems out of fear or anger, rather than looking at all your options and making an educated decision? If Patti had decided to quit immediately, she most likely would not have received a terrific reference and might have had a difficult time securing a new job. Fear and anger are two stumbling blocks for many people. In Chapter 2 we will discuss how to use these blocks to build your foundation rather than allow them to impede your forward progress.

Checklist for Moving On

	Yes	No
1. Have you completed the "Are You Living or Merely Surviving?" questionnaire?	____	____
2. Are you learning to accept where you are?	____	____
3. Have you reviewed your expectations?	____	____
4. Have you signed the agreement with yourself?	____	____
5. Have you reviewed how your intentions = your results?	____	____
6. Have you examined, listed, and revised your beliefs?	____	____
7. Have you reviewed your current comfort zone and agreed to stretch it from A to B?	____	____
8. Have you listed and read the steps you can take to accomplish your goals?	____	____

If you answered NO to any of these questions, you may be stuck or in fear. Turn to Chapter 2 to discover how to get free and move ahead. If you answered YES to all the questions, you are probably still asleep or in denial and fearful of the truth. Turn to Chapter 2 to learn how to move ahead. In fact, go to Chapter 2 right now as I don't know a single living person who has never experienced any fear. Fear can be a great motivator—let's learn how to use it to our best advantage!

▶ 2 ◀

Managing Change—
Instead of Letting
Change Manage You

The only thing that remains constant is change.
Anonymous

For years I struggled to avoid making any changes in my life. I was a creature of habit and liked the sense of security (even though it was a false sense of security) that I believed I had.

Would You Rather Be Right or Happy?

I recall an incident early on in my recruiting days that illustrates how much I abhorred change of any kind. Our division was growing and a new vice president was hired to expand the business. He had been very successful in his previous company, and we were excited to have him as our new leader. That is, until he suggested making a change. He had developed a new form to replace the one we used on a daily basis. He explained to us that by utilizing this new form (even though it took longer to complete than the old one), we would eventually save time and make more sales.

Well, I was outraged! Here we were busier than ever, and now we not only had to learn a new form that took longer to fill out, we didn't have any choice in the matter! I refused to comply. I made it known in no uncertain terms that I was very successful using the old form and I wasn't about to memorize a new one! (Luckily, I had a manager who knew me well and realized I was reacting out of fear.)

Rather than insist I change immediately, my manager was wise to allow me some time to get comfortable with the change. She suggested that I use the new form, but just fill in the information required on the old form. I reluctantly agreed. Within a couple of weeks I became familiar enough with the new form to complete it fully. Several months later I became the biggest advocate of this new form. Not only did I agree that it made my job easier, once I was promoted to manager, I used only the new form!

So why was I so resistant to change? Although I didn't realize it at the time, I was afraid and overwhelmed! When we are faced with change, we often sense a loss of control. We will do anything to hang onto the little bit of control we feel we have in life. My control was hanging onto the old form. I was more invested in being right than being happy. I became obsessed with being right. It was very important for me to convince my manager and others that changing the form would cause too many problems. As I grew more comfortable and resisted the change less, I became happier.

Are you resisting change right now? During the past several years the entire job scene has changed. Downsizing, rightsizing, reengineering, streamlining (gee, can I think of any more words to describe the corporate scene?), these words have dominated the headlines. The bottom line is there are more people and fewer jobs. Rather than embracing these signs of change as positive stepping stones, *we as a nation have become fearful and long for the good old days* where our fathers and grandfathers earned gold watches for their 25-year company anniversaries. Ask yourself, "**Would I rather be right or happy?**"

Before you can embrace the concept of "The New World of Work," which we will learn about in Chapter 4, we must first clarify where we are with our beliefs. Let's explore some of the beliefs that may be keeping you stuck in the past and how to let them go to move on to the present:

Evaluation: Are You Stuck in the Past?

	Yes	No
1. Do you find that when your mind wanders, you often relive past events or revisit past relationships?	____	____

Evaluation (*continued*)

	Yes	No

2. When you think of past events do you analyze how you should have done things differently? ____ ____

3. Do you mentally "beat up" on yourself after reviewing past events? ____ ____

4. Do you long for the good old days? ____ ____

5. Are you wary of new ideas or management changes in your company? ____ ____

6. Do you believe that you once had job security and now you don't? ____ ____

7. Do you play "what if" scenes in your mind and generally focus on the worst-case scenario? ____ ____

8. Have you avoided any major change in the past three years (i.e., in your job, home, personal appearance or habits, etc.)? ____ ____

9. If you do change anything, is it because you are forced to? ____ ____

10. Do you believe that although things are pretty messed up now, they will only get worse in the near future? ____ ____

If you answered YES to more than three questions, YOU ARE STUCK. The good news is that you can now acknowledge you're stuck. The other good news is that it isn't a permanent condition. *Remember, you are exactly where you are meant to be at this very moment.* Becoming stuck in the past is a protection from life (very similar to my being asleep for years). Now that you are aware of your situation, you can make a choice. . . . stay stuck or move on.

Should you decide to stay stuck in the past, you are welcome to do so. You may choose to set this book aside until you decide to move ahead. Otherwise you will feel like when you play Monopoly and go to jail, never getting to pass Go to collect $200. You'll only notice how much fun everyone else is having while you are stuck in jail. Or you could use your Get Out of Jail Free card and take your next turn. Either way, you are in the game.

For those of you who choose to move ahead into the present, this can be the turning point for you. Take a deep breath and relax. You are about to learn how to "live in the moment."

Learning to Live in the Moment

I can remember the exact moment I became aware I was "living in the moment." It changed my perception of everything. I was attending a seminar, and it was the first time I recall that my mind was focused 100% on the speaker and what he was saying. I wasn't thinking about the lunch break, or the room being too cold, or how I was going to manage to exit the room to go to the bathroom without being noticed. I realized then that I was living in the moment. Of course as soon as I realized it, I became so excited that I went right into the future (I couldn't wait to share what I had learned, so my thoughts became focused on my excitement rather than on what the speaker was saying).

When we live life in the past or future, we miss out on living. Only while living in the moment can you be totally "present" and participate. Otherwise we are only observing. Practice living in the moment. Take a look around you. Look at your hands and really observe them; become aware of your surroundings; allow yourself to fully absorb this moment in time. Then take the next few minutes to pay close attention to all your thoughts. These thoughts are called your *stream of consciousness*. Write these thoughts down as you are having them. When the time is up, review your list. Notice if your thoughts were in the past, present, or future. Isn't it interesting to note how many of your thoughts pertained to the past or future? This may help you to see how often we unknowingly allow our mind to wander.

Are you aware that your brain is a muscle? What happens to our muscles when we are inactive? They get flabby. When you allow your brain to wander and give it very little discipline or exercise, it becomes lazy. You may say to yourself, "But I can't help it, these thoughts just come into my mind." This is true only if you allow this behavior to continue. Should you decide to do anything differently, you must first be aware of what you are currently doing. **Each day pay attention to and write down your stream of consciousness.** These daily exercises will help you pay attention to what's going on in your mind. Once you make a commitment to staying in the present, ask your friends, family, and colleagues to assist you in staying on course. They can act as helpful reminders to you when you forget your new behaviors and get caught up in the *should haves* or fears of life.

Because I often work in my home office, I have the tendency to be in a work mode 24 hours a day. My daughter Caitlyn has been my greatest inspiration in learning to stay in the moment. One day in particular she was attempting to get my attention, and even though I was looking straight at her, she said to me, "Mom, where are you?" "I'm listening," I replied. "No, you're not. You always do this—say you are listening when you really aren't," she said in frustration. I proceeded to disagree with her until she said, "Okay, Mom, you be me for a while and I'll be you, then you can see what I mean."

I laughed and agreed to switch roles with her, but as soon as she began playing me, I was no longer laughing. "I do not do that!" I protested. "Yes, you do!" Caitlyn insisted. As I began to let her words sink in, I realized she was indeed right. As I've mentioned before and will talk about throughout this book, *children can be our greatest teachers.* Once I gained this new understanding about "staying present," my relationship with my daughters and family greatly improved. From time to time, I still find myself going "elsewhere," but the difference is that I have recruited my family and friends to gently remind me when I'm somewhere else. I'm now to the point where I can remind myself while in the midst of fading away.

Take some time to recall how you felt while doing the exercise on page 22. Notice that while you were in the moment you had no fear. *Fear only exists in the past or future.* When you allow yourself to be in the present moment, there is no room for fear.

Recently, I had the opportunity to put this concept to the test in probably the most important challenge of my life to date. My mother was diagnosed with terminal cancer, and I received a call to come spend the last days of her life with her. Although I had visited my mom a number of times during her illness, I was informed that she had lost a great deal of weight, and I was told not to be shocked. I had a few days to wrap up my work details before flying out to be at her side. Of course I spent those days not in the present but in the future. I attempted to prepare myself for what I was about to encounter by visualizing how I would react when I first saw her in that condition.

During that time I totally "got off track." (This happens to all of us at one time or another, so we'll discuss how to get back on track later in this chapter.) Fortunately, I had supportive people around me (they are my life coaches and have a mind-set similar to mine) who reminded me to stay in the moment. I was not only able to be with my mother during her last days, we were both able to enjoy those precious moments fully. At one time during her remaining days, I found myself jumping into the future (the unknown) and lamenting to the hospice aide that I wanted to know when we could expect her to die. He lovingly laughed and said to me, "Keep living your life and don't focus or try to predict such things. After all, you could die before she does!"

Because I was feeling overwhelmed and helpless, I was attempting to control any part of my life (and hers, I might add) that I could. When I realized how far I was out of the moment, I was able to bring myself back to reality and spend the remainder of the day and time with my mom, just being—not fearing.

All of us face death at some time in our life, but it doesn't have to take the loss of someone to determine whether we are in the moment or not. Losing a job or a way of life is a loss. We encounter many losses in our lives. If we spend the time in the loss and not the moment, we live in fear, not joy. When you can master this lesson, you have learned to reclaim your power.

Reclaiming Your Power

When you live in the moment, you are powerful! You can make good, sound decisions. When you are in the past or future, you make decisions from fear—fear of what has happened or fear of what will happen.

I once heard (and I wish I could give credit to whoever stated this—because it is brilliant—however, I can't recall who it was) that *the only thing we can truly count on in life is change.* Isn't that the truth? Although we can't often control what changes, we can control the way we view change. And when **we view change as the opportunity to grow and learn and experience the wonders of life, we have power.**

Are you empowered? Or have you given your power away to your spouse, your boss, or your children? Remember your new commitment to yourself from page 8? Repeat this commitment each and every day (several times a day) until you reclaim your power. When you find yourself slipping back into your old ways (and you will—trust me on that), be kind to yourself. You've just awakened from a coma, and you are learning to live all over again. Treat yourself gently, as you would a child who is learning to walk. Children tumble and fall many times before learning to run. Would you smack a child when he or she falls, or would you provide encouragement by hugging and letting the child know he or she will succeed next time?

Learning to accept this new world of work as we move into the millennium, you'll often feel like a child again. Can you recall how it felt to learn to tie your shoes or ride a bike for the first time? You made many mistakes along the way. And you learned from them. Remember learning to drive? Now you do it automatically. And some of us still have accidents. So prepare to make some mistakes along the way and not to always feel "okay" about where you are. *Only then can you make a decision either to get back to feeling good about yourself or to go in the other direction.*

> **Happiness is not a state to arrive at**
> **but, rather, a manner of traveling.**
> *Samuel Jackson*

Learning to Ask Yourself Questions

In order to make decisions that are for our highest good, we must learn to *ask ourselves the right questions.* Ask these simple questions before you take action of any kind:

1. Is this thought or action getting me closer to my goal or further away?
2. What are the possible consequences of my actions? Am I willing to take responsibility for my actions?
3. Am I taking this action for me or because someone else wants me to?
4. Am I making this decision or taking this action out of fear or power?
5. Am I using my intuition or am I acting purely from logic?

Getting Back on Track to Feeling "Okay" When You Get Sidetracked

Earlier I talked about my experience with my mom. I wasn't feeling very okay about anything. Even though I had a great excuse for not feeling good, I desired to feel better. I knew that if I desired to feel better, I must first be aware of and allow whatever feelings might surface. So I got angry (even though I knew it wouldn't bring her back); I allowed myself to feel sorry for myself (I set a time limit on this one); I lived in the past; I focused on the future holidays without her; and when I was all done with these feelings, *I made a choice to come back to the moment.*

And that is where you find me right now, writing these words to you. I chose to come back to the present where I feel the most joy (and I know my mom would be happy about this). I am sure there will be many times when I choose to forget and once again fall back into pain and sorrow. I will get through that as well, and so can you. Perhaps the purpose for my mom's death while I was writing this chapter was to encourage me to encourage you that if I can get through difficult times, so can you. Here are the steps I have used and currently am using to feel okay again:

1. Allow whatever feelings you have to surface. There are no right or wrong feelings. Feelings are not logical, and you don't have to justify them.
2. Express these feelings (to a confidant, friend, coach, journal, support group, etc.—whatever feels right to you).
3. Be kind to yourself. Kicking yourself when you are down will only cause more pain. Love yourself more and do one nice thing for yourself today.
4. Think of one thing that makes you special or a "good deal." If you can't recall one, ask someone who loves you to tell you one.
5. Turn to your faith (or higher being) and ask for help.

I have weeks when I feel great about myself, and then out of the blue—WHAM—I feel beat down. I used to stay down for a long time. You can choose to as well. However, I can tell you from firsthand experience it is a much more pleasant life when we *allow ourselves permission to feel good again,* to get back to having peace of mind. I believe life is as much fun as we make it, or as much work as we make it. So if you aren't having as much fun in your work or life as you desire, let's find out how you can.

Making Work Fun

Many years ago when I was a recruiter, I met a woman who had so much fun in her job I couldn't resist asking her how she was so successful. Kathleen laughed and said that she viewed life as a game and didn't take it very seriously. "But life is serious and so is work," I protested. (Even when I played board games as a child I took them very seriously. I never believed the old saying "It isn't whether you win or lose—it's how you play the game.") I had always believed it was serious business to play and the only fun came from winning!

Of course, after I got to know Kathleen and see firsthand how she lived her life and ran her business, I chose to learn what she knew. She offered me a job, and in return for her teaching me to have more fun in work, I agreed to teach her the recruiting skills I had learned. Not only did I have a great time working for her company, I made a lot of money and, after a couple of years, ended up purchasing her business! My new belief system is "The more fun you have, the more successful you will be."

Laughter Is the Best Medicine

According to Matt Weinstein, author of *Managing to Have Fun* (New York: Simon & Schuster, 1995), during the last decade there has been actual medical and scientific research to document that laughter and play can have a beneficial effect on your physical health. He states that during times of hearty laughter, your entire muscular system relaxes. Matt suggests looking at yourself in the mirror the next time you are laughing and noticing that your arms are limp and you have a contented smile on your face.

Other studies have shown that it *takes more facial muscles to frown than it does to smile.* When you are feeling tense and unhappy in your work environment or personal life, and you choose to feel better, practice the following: look in the mirror and smile. If you are feeling so rotten you find yourself having trouble even smiling, take two fingers, put one in each side of your mouth, and force yourself to smile. You will probably look silly and smile from this alone! The point here is don't wait to laugh or to feel better to get a smile. Give one first, and then you'll end up feeling happier.

Matt Weinstein has developed four principles of fun at work. "First, *think about specific people involved.* Even if you are not a manager, look to those around you whose daily life interacts with yours. Learn about these individuals. The more you know them, the more appropriate and effective you can be in using fun and play for reward, recognition, and revitalization. The second principle is to *lead by example.* Take some time to determine how comfortable you are with the idea of fun at work and then take actions on what you've learned.

If you're not getting personal satisfaction from what you're doing, it's not worth doing is the third principle. Don't kid yourself. You're not doing this just for your employee's or employer's benefit. You can choose this for yourself as well. The fourth principle is that *change takes time*. Be patient. A corporate culture (or personal one) doesn't change overnight. Start by planning a number of small events that give the clear message that you and the company are learning to celebrate yourselves."

Because I often work independently, I don't always have the opportunity to play or have fun with others. However, it doesn't take two to have fun. I have found ways to make myself laugh and have fun alone. I keep a joke book on my desk and funny pictures that make me smile. I have toys to play with (my favorite is called a Crdyl—a bunch of tiny magnets that I can arrange in creative ways). I use funny Post-it notes or humorous cards when attending to my correspondence. When I am tired of playing alone, I either arrange a meeting or telephone a business friend or colleague.

If your work environment is lacking fun, it's up to you to change it. Start small. *Pick one thing that you can do starting today to make your job more enjoyable.* Because we have gotten into habits of "working" rather than having fun, we must *plan* our fun. Take out your calendar, and for the next month, list one activity or action toward having fun each day. I guarantee, by the end of the month you will be enjoying your work more than you have in years!

Enjoying the Roller Coaster of Life

Do you close you eyes tight and yell furiously when the roller coaster takes a sharp dip? Or do you hold your hands high in the air, keep your eyes wide open, and enjoy the thrill of the intense ups and downs?

Life is like the ocean. The tide comes in, and it also goes out. Do you fight the tide or make adjustments for it?

When it rains, are you the kind of person that feels as though the day is ruined, or do you appreciate the gray day? Once again, you have choices. You can miserably decide that everything is ruined because the rain destroyed your plans, or you can choose to adjust your plans accordingly. My suggestion for success is to *accept that gray days will come and to learn to embrace them as easily as you would a sunny one.*

I once read that we should be thankful for the gray days in life (challenges, adversity, and the like). At the time, I couldn't fully understand this concept. I resisted being thankful as much as I resisted change of any kind. What I now fully comprehend is not only the meaning to being thankful for these gray days (by viewing them as opportunities for growth) but that I have the option to change my views when adversity hits. The steps to do this are similar to those used to getting back to being "okay" again found on page 26.

When challenges or adversity comes into our lives, we are often caught off guard. As in riding a roller coaster for the first time, we never know when or where the twists, turns, and plunges will occur. *Trying* to predict those times is pointless. Not only will we drive ourselves crazy by doing this, we will miss the enjoyment of living in the moment and fully experiencing the situation. Instead, I've found the way to live a more peaceful and full existence is to embrace positive attitudes about adversity. Ask yourself right now, "What are my beliefs about adversity?" Do you cringe at the very thought of it?

Several years ago when a particularly severe earthquake hit California, I remember seeing an interview on television with some of the individuals who were the hardest hit. (Often we refer to these people as victims or survivors; however, *a more empowered view is to see them as people who persist or carry on*). One man who was being interviewed really caught my attention. He owned a shop that sold only imported glassware. When the reporter questioned him about his losses and why he was in someone else's shop cleaning up instead of his own, he responded very matter of factly. He explained that this shopkeeper needed more help than he did at that very moment. When the reporter inquired about the damage to the glass shop, the owner admitted that he didn't have any insurance to cover the damages. "Isn't that awful," exclaimed the reporter. "How horrible!" she commented. What he said next both surprised me and inspired me deeply. "Well, I've learned one thing in this life. It's not so much what happens to us that matters, it's how we react to what happens that counts." He went on to say that he still had his health, no one was seriously hurt, and he could always rebuild.

As this owner stood in the ruins of his shop, with pieces of broken glass all around him, I thought how could he be so optimistic at a time like this? Suddenly a lightbulb went on in my head, and I truly understood for the very first time what I had done in the times of adversity and challenge in my own life. Rather than focus on my blessings (which were many), I had always focused on negative aspects of the challenge!

It never registered in my heart or mind when people told me that I must be positive or that I had a lot to be thankful for. (It only reminded me of how I felt when I didn't like lima beans as a child and my father made me eat them because I must be thankful for having food on the table. After all, there were starving kids in third world countries!) It seldom helped me assume a different attitude, and I usually resented the person giving such advice. So, *how do you get to a positive mind-set when you are feeling like a victim?*

First, take a piece of paper and draw a line down the center. On one side list every fear and concern you have about a particular challenge or situation. Keep writing until you can no longer think of anything else or are sick of feeling the fear. Next, on the other side write down all the good things you have in your life and all the good that can come as a result of this challenge. List the results as if all the "what ifs" worked out positively.

There is something about writing down our fears and concerns that helps us to realize how false they can be, or if we do have valid concerns, we can then make a plan of how to take action on them. Once we identify the fears, we can often get to the feelings behind them. For example, a couple years back I experienced a major cash-flow problem. I was planning to leave for vacation in a few days when I learned that a client was returning over $1,700 worth of merchandise. I had counted on this money to enjoy my vacation. My first thought (panic) was to cancel the vacation, which was something I didn't relish doing (my girls and I were really looking forward to this quality family time).

Once I recognized I was in the panic mode, I took some deep breaths, took out a piece of paper, and wrote down every concern, worry, and fear that I had. I kept writing until I had gotten it all out of my system. Then I wrote a list that included the best-case scenario. *What if I went on vacation and could still pay all my bills?* I would feel great. The panic subsided and I was then able to think clearly. I decided to go on the vacation anyway. I made an agreement with myself that if I went on the vacation, I wouldn't allow myself to worry the entire time and defeat the purpose of the vacation, which was to relax.

Well, we had one of the best vacations I can ever recall. I relished every moment with my girls, and they still talk about the fun we had. The Monday morning I returned to my office, I started to fear again. "What have I done? How will I pay my bills?" I asked myself. This time, however, I was able to stop myself before I got back into panic again. I simply said, "Vicki, STOP! Everything will work out fine; you had a great vacation, and you deserved it. All is well." I smiled to myself and felt better immediately. Shortly thereafter, the phone rang. It was the assistant to a professor at the University of Notre Dame. She explained that this professor was interested in purchasing my book to use as a text in teaching his students how to land a job. Marcia went on to ask if it was possible to order 80 copies of my book and Express-Mail a check to me the following day? I am seldom speechless; however, I was so overwhelmed by this good fortune, I could barely contain myself. Especially when I calculated the amount of the check for just about $1,700. Was this just a coincidence? Or a miracle?

When I hung up the telephone, I sat at my desk for several minutes and reflected on what had just happened. I realized how my thoughts had created my reality. Had I not gone on vacation and had I deprived myself and felt lousy about everything, perhaps I would not have received this call. I am not here to tell you how the universe works; all I know is that it works by *cause and effect*. I can only explain to you what steps I have used and how they have worked for me and hundreds of my clients. The results are astounding! I'll talk more about this mode of "prosperity consciousness" in Chapter 10. These are the steps I suggest for using your current reality to create your future reality:

Steps to Embracing Challenges, Changes, and Adversity and Moving Past Them

1. Ask yourself what your beliefs are and how you feel when you are presented with a challenge or adversity?
2. Truly accept that adversity is an on-going part of life and happens to everyone at one time or another.
3. Understand that avoiding pain often prolongs it. Give yourself time to "feel" your feelings. Even the painful ones.
4. Plan some time each and every day to "check in" with yourself and see what's really going on. Meditate or "journal."
5. Allow yourself time to daydream. Replace "What if it doesn't work out?" with "What if it does?"

6. Reinforce your positive thoughts by assuming whatever you desire to have happen is complete and you are just waiting to claim it.
7. Take an action toward this goal.
8. When you get sidetracked and slip into "old behaviors," acknowledge that you're temporarily stuck, forgive yourself, and move on.

It's important to remember that life is a *journey* not a destination. If you are only happy when things are going well, you may feel unhappy for a large chunk of your life. Everything in nature (including humans) has cycles. The seasons are cycles; the moon has cycles as does the tide. Do we attempt to control the moon or force the tide to come in? No, we understand how nature works and allow it to flow along.

Fighting or resisting something we have no control over doesn't make much sense. *All we have control over is how we view these events.* So it is with the roller coaster of life. We don't know how, when, or where the plunges and turns will come, and I don't know a person yet who claims to have all the answers. The only decision we truly have is whether we embrace these changes and move through them, or fight them endlessly. In the introduction to this book, I explained to those of you who may be "fighting," to lay down your sword. If you haven't done so yet, perhaps now is the time. By allowing yourself to give up some of your old "protections," and see things more clearly, you may be able to discover and start living your true purpose in life. After all, isn't that what we desire? To have a purpose and live it!

> **To love what you do and feel that it matters—**
> **how could anything be more fun?**
> *Katharine Graham*

Checklist for Moving On

	Yes	No
1. Did you take the "Are You Stuck in the Past?" evaluation?	____	____
2. Did you practice being in the moment and write down your "stream of consciousness"?	____	____

Checklist (*continued*)

	Yes	No
3. Did you role-play with a coworker, family, or friend on how they perceive you "being present"?	____	____
4. Have you "reclaimed your power" and reread your commitment to yourself from page 8?	____	____
5. Have you followed the steps to "getting back to okay"?	____	____
6. Did you incorporate some fun into your work and life?	____	____
7. Have you learned to accept change as a big part of your life and to embrace it?	____	____

► 3 ◄

Discovering Your Special Purpose

A person without a purpose is like a ship without a rudder.
Thomas Carlyle

Preparing to Discover Your Special Purpose

In Chapter 1 we learned about "trying" and why it doesn't work. In his book *Seven Spiritual Laws of Success* (San Rafael, CA: New World Library, 1994), Deepak Chopra explains that once we allow our uniqueness to shine through, we no longer have to try. Chopra says that when a bird flies, it isn't hard for them. However, the bird must flap his wings to gain the momentum to get off the ground. The bird understands his uniqueness and allows himself to experience it. We can choose to do the same to fully live our purpose.

Give Up Trying and Your Career Will Take Off

I admit that I never "tried" to write my first book; I just wrote it. Like Chopra's illustration of the bird who flaps his wings, I flapped and flapped until I gained enough momentum to fly.

After counseling thousands of job seekers over the years, I'm convinced that the *people who succeed in living their purpose are those who are willing to flap even though they don't have a written guarantee they can fly.* More often than not, the individuals who do not feel they are living their purpose fail because they refuse to risk taking any action until they are 100% convinced it will work. They never get that guarantee, so they never take the necessary actions.

There is no such thing as trying. *Trying* is just a word we use to make excuses for why we do not reach our goals. How often have you said to yourself or others when you didn't keep your commitment, "Well, I really tried!"

Pick up a pen or pencil right now. Try to throw it down. Now, are you still holding onto it? Or did you actually throw it? If you threw it down, pick it up, and do it again. If you are still holding onto the pen, are you still "trying" to throw it?

You either choose to hold onto it or choose to throw it; there is no inbetween. Remember this and you'll progress very quickly throughout your discovery of purpose. Are you willing to *commit* to discovering your purpose in life, or are you still saying "I'll give it a try?" For those who are truly committed to reaching their destination and will not take no for an answer, let's proceed.

Committing to Purpose

Every single thing in our world has a purpose—including inanimate objects. Rocks serve several purposes. Centuries ago humans used rocks to start fire, to build shelters, and so on. We soon discovered that rocks could be polished and made into beautiful jewelry and gemstones. Many individuals believe that rocks have energy. Crystals are used in healing. Diamonds are used to express love. They have a purpose. Just like a rock that indeed has energy, so do you. You might require some chipping, polishing, and buffing to see your shine, but nonetheless, at your core-self you have reason to shine and a purpose for being here on this earth.

In Chapters 1 and 2, we've learned how to identify some of our protections that prevent us from being who we really are. We've also started the process of stretching our comfort zones and embracing change. All these steps are necessary in order to commit to discovering our special purpose in life. **In order to discover what you desire to do in life, you must be willing to discover what you aren't willing to do!** You must make the commitment to discover your purpose without having a *written guarantee* that whatever you attempt will be your ultimate purpose.

This is where your faith or inner-knowingness comes into the picture. As you allow yourself to "be" you will begin to notice a voice that is not your protections or beliefs speaking, but, instead is your intuition. This intuition will carry you through the process of living in purpose, even though it may not make logical sense. However, you must choose to commit to the discovery process first and have faith before you can begin to hear your inner-voice or intuition with complete clarity.

I remember when I first learned about Christopher Columbus in grade school. We were taught that he was told that the world was flat. Even though the world believed this to be true, he made the journey anyway. Why would he do that? Why would he risk his life and the lives of those on his ship to discover the unknown? Did he have a death wish? *Or was his faith so strong and his intuition so keen, he was willing to take the risk?* Had he waited for a guarantee that he would not sail off the edge, would we know America as we do today? You don't have to take the risk that Christopher Columbus took in order to discover your purpose; *however, you must be willing to learn to commit to the process, learn to listen to your intuition again, and then take appropriate action.*

Perhaps you choose to make a fire in the fireplace. You wouldn't look to the fireplace and expect to have a fire first and only then feed it wood, right? Of course you wouldn't. Otherwise, you'd probably stand there and freeze while waiting. The same principle applies to discovering your purpose—you must take action first, then be warmed by the fire of your efforts.

Living in Purpose Is Like Gardening

We all know that in order to grow a beautiful garden, it takes a great deal of time and nurturing for it to pay off. First, you must know what you desire your garden to look like (visualize your ideal career and focus). Next, you can decide to research which plants and flowers will grow best in your soil (research at the library what industries and positions you may have an interest in and choose to pursue). After that, you must prepare the earth to receive the seeds or plants (uncover leads in your field). Then comes the actual planting (make your calls and set up informational interviews). Without water and sun and loving attention, your new little seedlings will die (make your follow-up calls and nurture the leads and contacts along). If you take all the above steps, barring any natural interruptions (hurricanes, etc.), you'll soon have a bountiful harvest of flowers and plants (job offers).

The problem many individuals face when searching for purpose is that they would rather be out in the garden, smelling the beautiful flowers, than taking the necessary steps to achieve one. However, most gardeners agree that a shortcut in any of the steps will surely result in a sorry-looking garden.

Is your career full of weeds? If so, take a good long look at how you can do it differently. Have you taken shortcuts? Are you *trying* to rush the process? In *Seven Spiritual Laws of Success* Deepak Chopra explains that in order to achieve career happiness and success, we can choose to be more process oriented, rather than focusing on the results. So if you are experiencing difficulty in discovering what your purpose is or having a tough time with your current position, start by focusing on the **process** *of getting what you desire* rather than on what you desire. **Write down at least three ways that you are getting value from your current situation.** Perhaps you are between jobs and can't see anything good about your current situation. Is this time off giving you time to reflect on what you really desire in your career? That's a value. Have you been able to spend more time with your friends and family? That's another value. Keep going and come up with three benefits to your current situation.

For many of us, we believe we are committed to purpose and doing things differently; however, we often find ourselves somewhere between commitment and results—in limbo. *We find ourselves wishing, hoping, and praying things will be different without taking any action or exhibiting any new behaviors.* When this occurs, we find ourselves in limbo—wanting our life to be better, but still wavering back and forth between old and new attitudes.

The Limbo Stage

Being in *limbo is not liking what you have and not quite being at the point to do things differently.* It is by far the most painful of all the stages of life, and yet this is where many of us spend most of our time. I must have really liked being in limbo because I spent much of my adult life there. I lived in limbo for years before committing to a divorce. I also spent much of my career life in limbo as well.

Nothing is really work unless you would rather be doing something else.
James M. Barrie, English writer, 1860–1937

After going to the Understanding Yourself and Others seminar and committing to my dream of writing my book, I was excited and full of enthusiasm. However, shortly thereafter, my whole world changed! The bottom dropped out of the recruiting industry, and I couldn't make a placement to save my life! No placements meant no commissions. No commissions meant no money. I was broke! I sold all my possessions of value, advertised for a roommate to share expenses, and had garage sales to make some money. Eventually things got so bad financially, I moved back to my father's home, my two girls in tow.

Humiliated, broke, and in despair, I wondered why this was happening to me. Wasn't I in search of a better life? Wasn't I pursuing my dream? What happened to "do what you love and the money will follow?" How could it get much worse? Well, it did!

I took a position outside the recruiting industry (just to get a regular paycheck) and hated every moment of it. I worked 12 to 14 hours per day for a boss whose management style revolved around a vocabulary of four-letter words. I never saw my kids, my bills were mounting, and I felt like an 18-year-old again living in my father's home.

One day as I was sitting in a management meeting, I began to experience the most horrible feeling. I felt as though I was being sucked into a large black hole—a vortex. I sat in this rather long meeting very quietly. (Usually the other staff members couldn't get a word in edgewise.) I decided during this meeting that I could no longer continue working at this company. Their philosophy of doing business went against every moral value that I had. I could no longer let myself succumb to working somewhere just to make a dollar and at the risk of losing my integrity and sanity.

After the meeting ended, I asked my director to meet with me in my office immediately. Sensing something was wrong, she agreed. Shortly after she closed the door to my office, I looked her dead in the eyes and said, "Today will be my last day." As I said these words, I felt a freedom that I had not felt for a long time. What I really meant was today was the last day I would sell myself short.

You would think that being 33 years old, I wouldn't care what my father thought. Wrong. As I drove home, my old fears resurfaced. Was I crazy? What had I done? I had no money, no job, and now I had to go home and tell my dad that I had quit my job. A single mom with two kids should be more responsible, right? Well, yes and no. Hindsight is always 20/20, isn't it? Soon after, much to my father's dismay, and after months of agonizing pain, I filed for bankruptcy.

The purpose of my sharing this information with you is not to gain your sympathy but to help you learn from my pain. *You don't have to lose everything, however, in order to live your purpose and realize your dreams.* You have a choice. I didn't know this at the time. I believed that if I had nothing to lose, then the only way I could go was up. I now know that I can have it all. You can, too! Once I learned that I could live my purpose without leaving my job and becoming a starving artist, I was on my way! I decided to recommit to my purpose.

Recommitting to Purpose

While in my limbo stage I volunteered to assist at the Understanding Yourself and Others seminar. The facilitator was engaged in a conversation with a man, Scott, regarding what he was doing with his life. Scott explained that he had a half-written book on coping with divorce, but he never got around to finishing it. The facilitator asked why he had not completed it. Scott shrugged his shoulders and said that he guessed it wasn't that important to him. Tracey (the facilitator) looked at Scott in shock. "Not that important!" she exclaimed. "Well, it is important to me. I went through a horrible divorce last year, and I sure could have used your advice. Because you are not committed to your dream, I had to miss out!"

Tracey quickly scanned the room and said, "How many others in here have half-written books?" I somehow knew she was referring to me. Tentatively, I raised my hand and admitted that I did. "What is the book about?" she questioned. "Getting hired in the '90s," I replied. Tracey said, "Well, I sure could have used that book as well, because I also needed to find a job after my divorce." Quietly she spoke, "People, don't you see—it's your obligation to live your dream. By selling out on yourselves you affect the lives of many others. If you won't do it for you—won't you do it for the rest of us?"

That night I went home and dusted off my manuscript and recommitted to my goal. I realized then that because of my fears I had not been willing to do whatever it took to follow my dream. I had been more invested in protecting myself and staying in my comfort zone than I was in living my purpose. It was a sad realization at first, and then it empowered me to do things differently, but first I decided to let go of my past in order to create a better future.

Letting Go of the Past to Create a Brighter Future

Once you've discovered how to slow down a bit and allow yourself to be, you can progress to removing some of the layers you've built up over the years that may be covering your true self.

As we grow up, we learn to protect ourselves from being hurt. Have you ever eaten an artichoke? If you haven't, you don't know what you are missing. The outer leaves are tough and prickly, yet as you get closer to the heart of the artichoke, the leaves become tender and sweet. The heart is covered by very thin leaves called the choke (this protects the heart). However, when you carefully scrape away the inedible portion (the choke), you are left with the most delicious morsel of food imaginable (other than chocolate, of course!)—the heart. Now, picture yourself with years of these hard, protective leaves around you and your heart and give yourself permission to peel them off, one by one. Be patient, this takes some time, but it's worth it. One of the first tiny steps that you can take to live your purpose and reveal your true self is to become aware of your protections.

Becoming Aware of Protections That Are Keeping You Stuck

Let's examine some common protections we've built up over the years that prevent us from pursuing our dreams. One of my protections was to pretend that I had all the answers; this protected me from my fear of being wrong and then rejected. By assuming a false bravado and intimidating people into "seeing my way," I was able to fool myself into believing that I was right and they were wrong. (I was choosing to be right rather than happy!)

Being right made me feel powerful and in control. This false sense of control kept me from experiencing good relationships, a satisfying career, and inner peace. *Fear is the root of all false need for protection.* By feeling afraid of failure or success, by fearing intimacy and rejection, I learned to become a very good actress. Or at least I thought I was at the time.

Looking back now, I probably didn't fool too many people; they just didn't confront me on it due to their own issues. Perhaps they were afraid of conflict, or fearful that I would turn it around and call them on an issue with which they were having trouble. So we walk around *trying* very hard (notice I use the word "trying" here—not do-ing) to avoid really looking at ourselves, or at others for that matter, focusing most of our energies on protecting ourselves. Take a look at the following list of common protections and circle those that apply to you (be honest: cheating on this is like cheating at solitaire; al-though no one else will know, you will):

Laughing or making a joke when really you are hurting.
Anger.
Shyness.
Shouting over other people to be heard.
Fidgeting.
Acting.

Add to this list as you think of more ways that you've protected yourself in this world.

How to Control Your Emotions
Rather Than Letting Your Emotions Control You

Now that you're aware of how you protect yourself, you can decide if these protections are serving you. If they are no longer serving you (and chances are they aren't, or you would be happily involved in a career that you love), you can decide if you are willing to learn a new way.

You must make a conscious decision to accept this fact: *If you keep doing what you're doing, you'll keep getting what you're getting.* If you no longer like what you're getting, you can choose to learn to change what you are doing. For example, when I realized that one of my biggest protections was anger, I was then able to decide to substitute for the anger something that would serve me better: forgiveness.

First, I learned that I am in charge of my emotions, rather than my emotions controlling me. This was scary to me. I could no longer be the victim of my feelings; instead I had the opportunity to be accountable for my actions and feelings. At first, you may resist the italicized statement in the last paragraph—I know I did. I used to believe that people made me feel a certain way and I couldn't help that I got angry or hurt. *All anger truly results from other people doing things differently than we do.* If we all behaved in the same exact fashion, there would be no reason to get angry. However, the world would be a very boring place!

For years I had been angry with my ex-bosses, dad, mom, sister, brother, ex-husband, friends, and so on. When I was young, I was taught that anger was bad. When I got angry, I was usually sent to my room. I was told, "If you can't say something nice, don't say anything at all." What I learned from my childhood experiences was to keep my anger inside and smile. My experiences turned into my beliefs. I believed that it was not acceptable to express anger. I also believed that I must smile and pretend that all was okay, even when it was not. I learned to cover up my anger so well that by the ripe old age of 26 I was diagnosed with an ulcer. My anger was literally eating me up!

So I decided to learn a new way to deal with my anger and other feelings that I had become the victim of. Instead of pretending they didn't exist, I now give myself permission to feel whatever I'm feeling. For example, when I get angry (yes, I still get angry, although not nearly like I used to), I allow myself five minutes to get as angry as I choose (without violence, of course!). I may punch a pillow or write down all my angry feelings until the anger begins to dissipate. I give myself five minutes to manage these feelings and really feel them. Typically, after only a few minutes, I am able to return to a peaceful state of mind. If I am still angry or hurt after these five minutes, I'll continue the process until I'm feeling centered again.

When I'm depressed I give myself 24 hours to feel as depressed as I desire, and then I prepare myself to wake up the following morning and "let go of it." By allowing myself to feel, instead of pushing my feelings deep inside, I've gained several benefits. My health is better than it has been in years. I no longer feel like a walking time bomb ready to explode at any moment. I don't get into an automobile and lose control in traffic jams. My relationships, both at work and home, have improved dramatically, and best of all, I like myself better. Once *you are able to give yourself permission to feel, you start to notice that you, not your emotions, are in control.*

It is important to note that people often mistake "living in purpose" as living happily ever after. This simply is not true. All people feel a variety of emotions and feelings. Even though I love what I am involved with in my career, I still experience every emotion imaginable. The difference, however, is that when you stay centered in your purpose, you maintain peace of mind alongside all your feelings and emotions.

Before I could replace my old belief that anger was bad with a new, positive belief, I had to make a choice to clear away any past residue. In other words, I decided it was time for a tune-up!

Changing Your Own Oil
(Give Yourself a Tune-Up for a Smoother Ride)

Every three months like clockwork, I go into the fast-lube shop and get an oil change for my car. Why? So it runs well and won't break down. I wish we had fast-lube shops for humans! If we compared our emotional oil tank to the oil tank of a car, we would see that we could all benefit from an oil change! You can't just add new cans of fresh oil to a tank that is filled to the brim with old, gunky sediment and expect that to work miracles. First, you must drain the old oil and get rid of it; then you can add the new oil. The following exercises are designed to get you ready for adding some new oil to your tank.

To learn how to deal with anger in a healthy way, I suggest saying this affirmation daily: "I have a right to feel anger; anger is not bad unless I react to it badly. Anger directed in the proper way is powerful. I allow myself to feel whatever I feel and not to judge it as good or bad, or right or wrong."

Next, write letters to whomever you are angry with. Get in a comfortable space where you will not be interrupted, get a pad of paper, and allow yourself to feel your anger. Write down your feelings to this person without checking grammar, punctuation, or spelling. These letters won't be mailed, so let out all your true feelings. Keep writing until you no longer feel the anger. When you are finished, take the letter and tear it up and throw it away. Burn it in the backyard grill! Get rid of it.

Keep writing the letters until you can't write any longer. You may also choose to write a letter to yourself. Often, we hold the most anger in reserve for ourselves. Once you let go of your anger (the old, thick oil that makes you sluggish), you can more readily claim your own personal power and unique purpose.

After this process, you may feel relieved, sad, depressed, guilty, or happy! Whatever feelings you have at this time are okay. Allow yourself to feel these feelings. Don't judge them as right or wrong. Feelings aren't logical, are they? Sometimes we aren't sure why we feel the way we do. It may help you to discover the why behind what you are feeling, and you may decide to see a counselor or therapist to work out some long-standing feelings. However, for now it's important to learn how to express your feelings again.

For years I felt numb. All that smiling on the outside while inside I was in a rage left me unsure about how I truly felt. My biggest fear was that if I allowed my feelings to come out, I would have to be carted off in a white jacket! So I kept my feelings under tight wraps and tried to shove them further and further down, but they surfaced in illness after illness, divorce, and bankruptcy. I became so filled with anger that I felt worthless. It goes without saying that people who feel worthless attract more of the same. When I was able to let go of the anger and stop attacking myself long enough to get a glimpse of some of my beauty, my life changed. So can yours!

TIP Here are a few ways of learning to deal with anger constructively: Sit or lie on your bed and punch your pillow until you no longer feel angry. Learn how to silent-scream. To do so, scream as loud as you can but don't use your voice (great for at work). Give yourself a limit on how long you choose to be angry (five minutes); be as angry as you can in those five minutes without hurting yourself or others. As soon as you allow yourself to be angry, the anger usually starts to dissipate. It's only when we "try" not to feel our anger or emotions that we feel out of control. When we give ourselves permission to feel them, we maintain control!

We can learn to deal effectively with our feelings; however, without forgiveness you will leave an empty void. *Forgiving those people whom you perceived as having hurt you is not for their benefit but for your own peace of mind!*

Forgiveness: The Secret to a New Way of Life

According to the *Webster's II New Riverside Dictionary*, to forgive means "to pardon or absolve, to stop being angry about or resentful against." Saying "I forgive you" may seem difficult to do at first; however, when you realize the benefits you gain from forgiveness, and practice it daily, you will see dramatic results!

When I was able to release some of my anger and realized just how much I was hurting myself, I made a decision to quit abusing myself. Forgiveness is not about others, for your anger doesn't hurt them nearly as much as it hurts you. Instead, *forgiveness is an act of kindness that you give to yourself.*

Exercise: Forgiveness

Get in a comfortable position (be sure to take any phones off their hook and anticipate any distractions prior to getting started). *Begin by taking five deep breaths.* Close your eyes and picture yourself in a place you really enjoy (example: in the mountains, near a babbling brook, where the sky is blue and the breeze is warm). Allow yourself to picture this scene in your mind's eye. (You may not be able to see anything initially; however, with practice you will improve.) Let your imagination be free to create a safe and loving environment for you. Invite the person you would like to forgive to join you. Have him or her sit near you where you can look into each other's eyes. Repeat the following statements: "I forgive you for _____" (fill in the blank with whatever you choose to forgive the person for). "I know it was not your intention to hurt me. I know that you did the best you could with the knowledge you had. I forgive you and set you free." Perhaps you'd like to ask for this person's forgiveness as well. Now is the time. "I ask you to forgive me for any pain that you feel I caused you. I ask you to forgive me and set me free." You may decide to have a conversation with this person at this time; if so, keep in mind this isn't about being right or wrong; you are just here to forgive.

This exercise can be done with anyone you'd like, including yourself! (Even if you have a friend or relative who has passed away, this may be a good time to tell that person anything you did not take the opportunity to say when he or she was with you.) After you've said what you decided to say, allow yourself to say goodbye to this person and your surroundings and focus your attention on coming back into the room. You can go back as many times as you wish. I use this exercise on an ongoing basis in my life. It keeps me very centered, focused, and able to maintain peace of mind.

The healing process of forgiveness is ongoing. We may never forget the past events that have hurt us; however, we have a choice to either use them as an excuse for not succeeding in our purpose, or we can use these experiences to enhance our purpose. (I will never forget the devastating experiences of the past five years; however, I value what I've learned from this adversity, and I'm using what I've learned to assist you now.)

After you've allowed yourself to forgive and have practiced doing so, you are ready to move forward. Quite often we can benefit a great deal when we allow ourselves to grieve for our past and over the old wounds that we've held onto for so long. Learning to *move through this sadness* will open you up to experience much happiness and peace of mind in your life. Forgiveness is the catalyst for allowing yourself to receive all the wonderful joys that living your purpose will bring.

You've already learned that forgiveness is the key to progressing toward your purpose. Once you have forgiven yourself for all your imperfections, you are free to see *how perfect you really are*. Many people feel that when we forgive ourselves for our past actions or guilt that we are letting ourselves "off the hook" and giving ourselves or others permission to continue the behaviors that hurt us. Actually, the opposite is true. Forgiveness frees you from the guilt that keeps you stuck. People who are stuck in guilt, blame, or shame often go into depression. *Depression* is anger focused inward and depletes us of energy. When we lack energy, we often become lazy and repeat the cycle of unhealthy behavior. On the other hand, *individuals who truly like themselves, are willing to take responsibility for their actions, and learn from their mistakes find they have a great deal of energy and enthusiasm*. Once you start using such energy toward the positive goal of "being in purpose," instead of directing it toward anger and resentment, you will begin to discover who you really are and listen to your intuition.

Learning to Trust Your Intuition

I think most of us are looking for a calling, not a job. Most of us, like the assembly-line worker, have jobs that are too small for our spirit. Jobs are not big enough for people.
Studs Terkel, *journalist*

After you have learned to go inside and become quiet for awhile, you'll be able to begin to hear what your true self desires to tell you. Call it your intuition, your higher power, God, or your inner-voice, this voice will only be heard when you allow it to be. *This voice will not override your own free will.* You may choose to give this voice permission to be heard again, especially if you haven't paid attention to it in years. Do you remember having the time as a child to lie on the fresh-mowed grass and gaze up at the clouds and experience this timeless expression of peace? If you've never had the opportunity to experience this, I highly recommend that you do so. This kind of peace allows us to get in touch with our inner-voice and who we really are.

As adults, we can learn a wealth of information from children. Children have not yet forgotten their inner-voice and rely on it regularly to keep them feeling safe. Have you ever asked a child to give someone a hug whom they don't feel comfortable with? They just won't do it. They rely on their inner-voice to tell them when it's okay to feel comfortable. Dogs do it, kids do it, yet adults seem to think we've outgrown it. I disagree. Whenever I have a major decision to make, or choose to hear the answer to a problem I'm facing, I turn to my inner-voice for guidance. My life is much more peaceful and prosperous as a result of doing just this.

Now, don't think because you've meditated once or twice that all the answers will come to you immediately. Some individuals require more time. Others will feel comfortable right away. *Remember, you are exactly where you are meant to be right now, no further ahead or behind.*

Why do you think the story of *The Wizard of Oz* is still as popular today as it was 50 years ago? The movie has a message for all of us. Dorothy spent the entire time facing life's perils in search of a way to get home. She finally discovered she had the power all along but didn't know it! *You have the power, too,* and now that you know it, *what will you do with it?*

My Journey to Fulfilling My Purpose

Once I recommitted to my dream, I took some odd jobs and worked on my book. Little by little my self-esteem improved, and I felt that my life was going to work out after all.

When love and skill work together, expect a masterpiece.
John Ruskin, English writer, 1819–1900

Miracles aren't always well defined and wrapped in sunshine. Often they come cloaked in the *disguise* of perceived pain. So it was with the following months of my life. Leaving my job was the last straw that prompted my dad to ask me to find a new place to live. I was completely devastated by this. I felt betrayed by my own father and as helpless as a child. I didn't think it was humanly possible to cry as much as I cried during that time. It wasn't until a year or so later I came to realize that although I judged this time in my life as "the worst thing that ever happened," *these experiences provided key lessons I was meant to learn and use later on in life.*

As I think back, had I stayed longer in the comfort of my father's home, I probably would not have finished my book, or felt good enough about myself to have the courage to begin to complete it. Instead, I frantically contacted an old friend and asked if I could move into her house for a few months. I am thankful she agreed. I began working again for an ex-employer, Kathleen, in the recruiting business. Soon after, she decided to marry and offered to sell me her business. I wanted to buy the business very much, but I wasn't in a financial position to do so. Kathleen was marrying a man who was financially well-off, and to my amazement, she offered to sell me her business for one dollar. (Once you realize you are worthy of receiving, and also that you don't have to fulfill your special purpose all alone, miracles become everyday events! We'll further explore the prosperity attitude in Chapter 10.) She also encouraged me to finish my book and supported me, both emotionally and financially, through this transition. The friend I was staying with also helped me get back on my feet (with both a place to stay and money), and I was soon able to get a place of my own and finish my book.

After completing my book, I went in search of a publisher. Although I had some encouraging rejections ("Your book looks good, but we just did a career book"), I was not able to secure a publisher. It would have been easy to give it all up at this point. It would have been easy to tell myself that at least I had finished my book. However, by this time, I had been through so much I remained committed to my dream. I decided to learn all I could about self-publishing! Over the next six months, I read every book on the subject of publishing and called every author and publisher who might talk to me. I ate, slept, and dreamt about my book.

I encouraged my girls to be patient with me, and we all agreed that once my book was accepted in the bookstores, we'd go to Disney World. We pasted posters of Mickey Mouse all over the house to keep ourselves motivated. Every week I visited the local bookstores, gazed in the windows, and visualized my book among those in the store window display. I would tell myself over and over again that someday my book would be right alongside those books. When I purchased a book from the store, I would engage the clerks in conversation and tell them about my book. At first they were impressed; however, when they asked me who the publisher was and I told them I hadn't found one yet, they usually rolled their eyes or looked away and murmured, "That's nice." I didn't care, though (well, maybe just a little), because I knew someday they would take me seriously.

No One Can Take Your Dream from You

In the movie *The Shawshank Redemption*, Tim Robbins's character is in prison. Explaining to a fellow inmate why he still had hope and why the prison officials couldn't get the best of him, he says, "They can't get inside of me. It's in here," pointing to his heart. "They can't get to it." *Once you realize your specialness and purpose is internal, not external, nothing anyone says or does will affect you.* No one can touch it!

After months of preparation to get some publicity for my upcoming book, I finally got a call from a local newspaper in the suburbs of Chicago. They agreed to run a short piece about a local author. I was in seventh heaven! You'd have thought that someone had just told me I had won the lottery!

The day finally approached for the story to run, and I was out at the newsstands at dawn to purchase 15 copies of the newspaper. I could barely get back to the car before tearing apart the paper looking for my article. It was such a short piece that I had to look through the entire paper several times before I even found it. I raced through the article quickly, and when I was finished, I came to the shocking realization that they had forgotten to include the title of my book. The paper had referred to my years of effort as "her book." My heart stopped momentarily, and I was totally disappointed.

I drove home near tears and proceeded to call the writer to let him know what had happened. After several attempts, I finally reached him and told him my concerns. He apologized and agreed to run a follow-up blurb in a few days or weeks, although he couldn't promise when it would appear.

Still, I was excited about getting my first break into print, and I went about my daily work toward getting the book printed. A few days later, I received a call from a local college that I had worked with regarding career issues. (The college was mentioned in the article about me.) A woman from the college explained that since people didn't know the name of the book, they were calling the school to try to locate it. I was thrilled. Especially when she told me that Barnes & Noble had called and wanted me to do a book signing!

I called Barnes & Noble immediately and spoke with its public relations coordinator. She informed me that although she didn't know the name of my book, what I had to say seemed interesting. And would I like to do an event in approximately six weeks? (Another miracle?) Of course I readily agreed, although I didn't even have the book printed yet and I was set to leave for Disney World in four weeks (my reward for completing the book).

I quickly arranged for the book to be printed and went to work on editing the final manuscript and designing a book cover. Up to this point, I'd been selling the book in a spiral-bound version and hadn't a clue as to how to get a book bound and ready for bookstore sales.

During this commotion, the woman I had hired to type the manuscript told me that she could no longer make any revisions because of her busy schedule in her day job. Well, you guessed it! I ran out, purchased a computer, and taught myself how to work it in 24 hours! The rest of the six weeks are pretty much a blur to me now. I recall working until three o'clock in the morning most days. I'd sleep for two to four hours, get up, and do it all over again. I was determined to not only get the book finished in time but go on vacation as planned. The night before we left, I instructed the printer to overnight a sample of the book to me in Florida so that I could give him the go-ahead to print the first 1,000 copies.

My daughters and I had a great trip and a much-desired rest. In fact, without this time off to recoup, I don't think I could have made it through the next few months.

My first book signing was a terrific success. Barnes & Noble was excited about my book sales and referred me to a sister store in the area, and I did an event there as well. Soon, Barnes & Noble was one of my best customers!

Shortly after my initial book signing, I talked to a gentleman who owned a career-book publishing house on the east coast. He patiently explained to me that although my book had potential, it would never sell to any of the large book chains. He went on to tell me that he had more than 12 years' experience in career-book publishing and stores would not buy from self-publishers. I listened carefully while he continued recounting his reasons why my project couldn't work until I politely interrupted him to explain that although I understood his reasoning, Barnes & Noble had already purchased 500 copies and was currently selling them. Sounding somewhat surprised, he went on to tell me that this was a fluke and not to count on much more than that. I recall thanking him kindly for his honesty and, near tears, hanging up the phone.

My assistant became very nervous and told me that if someone with his credentials was that negative, perhaps I had better listen to him. For the very first time since starting the project, I felt more than doubt. I felt fear—immobilizing fear. Not only was this man against me, but now my loyal friend and assistant didn't believe in me any longer. I told her that if she no longer believed that my book was the very best career book available in the marketplace, she would no longer be able to sell it. It was that simple. We are all our hardest sale. *If we are not sold on ourselves, we cannot persuade others.* My world was falling apart. Again. My assistant gave her notice two days later, and I was once more on my own.

The only advice I decided to listen to from my peer career publisher on the east coast (for which I am very grateful) was this: "The only way you will survive in publishing is by becoming an excellent marketer." So I did. I joined the Publishers Marketing Association (PMA) and read every newsletter it published, from cover to cover. Twice.

One gloomy afternoon as I was contemplating how to make ends meet, I received a fax. The fax was announcing a contest sponsored by PMA that was designed especially for small publishers wanting a national distributor. The contest deadline was in 24 hours, and in order to qualify, I would need to overnight two copies of my book with a check for $50.

At this particular time I could barely pay my rent, let alone spare $50 and the cost of overnighting or express-mailing my package to them. I spent the next few hours debating my next step. After several agonizing hours, and relying heavily on my intuition, I decided to go for it!

Three weeks later I received a certified letter stating that my book had been selected (by a panel of experts from Waldenbooks, Barnes & Noble, and other major players in the publishing field) as one of the "top ten small press books." By being selected, I was automatically given the opportunity for national distribution by three major book distributors. I read this letter 17 times before it actually set in.

Six months later my book became available in bookstores throughout the nation. (Even bookstores in Canada were ordering!) I appeared on several hundred radio stations and was selected to be a "career strategist" for CNBC's *Career Television Network*. I began writing several career columns and articles for newspapers and magazines across the country.

Shortly thereafter, Dearborn Publishers spotted an article I wrote and pursued me to buy the rights to my book and release a second edition. In September of 1994 we finalized an agreement, and in the spring of 1995 the book was rereleased under Dearborn's imprint. I had finally gotten what I desired all along: to get my book published for the purpose of educating individuals on how to get hired in the '90s. I just did it in a roundabout way! I had trusted in my purpose and *focused on the process not the outcome*. My faith, energy, and perseverance had finally paid off.

In order to discover your purpose and make doing so a manageable process, I'd like to share with you many of the steps, ideas, and tips that I learned during my transition. I hope that by following some of my suggestions, you can learn from my mistakes and pain, and you'll be able to enjoy your discovery as much as possible. I found that during this process I "tried" too hard! My career as an author began to flourish when I *got out of my own way long enough to let things happen*.

Now that you know you are exactly where you are meant to be, you can take the weight of the world off your shoulders. You can stop trying and learn how to be.

Relearning How to Be a Human BEing— Not a Human DOing

When I finally "got" that I was exactly where I was meant to be in my life (up to this point), *I realized that all the occurrences in my life that I perceived as bad actually were not*.

It wasn't until a couple of years ago that I began to understand that if my life had been the white-picket-fence kind, I could not possibly have fulfilled my life's purpose. How could I know what you (the reader) are going through unless I experienced it first? It would be like trying to explain what riding a horse was really like without ever riding one. *When I truly understood that all the experiences we have in life are for a reason* (whether we deem them good or bad at the time they are happening) was when my purpose and dream manifested itself.

Learning how to be will take practice. Yes, I said practice. Now you might say, "Vicki, you are contradicting yourself. You just explained that all we have to do is be. You are right; I did say that. But you see, we as a nation are out of the practice or habit of "being." We really never learned how! We've always been taught to "do" our whole lives. If that's what we should be doing, why aren't we called "human doings" instead of "human beings?" We are rather rusty at the art of being a "human being" and, therefore, require some practice. A great book with helpful ideas on how to be is *Don't Just Do Something Sit There* by R. Eyre (New York: Simon & Schuster, 1994). It's filled with exercises and antidotes on relearning the art of living without all the "shoulds" and stress we've grown accustomed to dealing with in life.

Exercise: Learning to "Be"

Are you ready to begin learning how to be? Great. Get in a comfortable spot (without television, phones, people, etc., to interrupt you). Start by inhaling deeply while mentally counting to five. When you get to five, hold the breath for five counts. Next, exhale slowly while counting to five. Repeat this procedure five times or until you start feeling relaxed.

For the next five minutes just allow yourself to be. As soon as a thought comes to your mind, allow it to disappear by breathing into the thought. Allow yourself to enjoy the silence and how wonderful it feels to experience "peace of mind." (For those just beginning meditation or relaxation, you may be frustrated by the "stream of consciousness" that keeps interrupting your peace of mind. Have patience and realize that learning to be at peace takes discipline, time, and practice.)

If after these five minutes you are still feeling "wound up," take a piece of paper and write out every thought that comes into your mind for the next few minutes. This "stream of consciousness" goes on continuously until we recognize it and learn to channel our energies elsewhere. By writing and allowing these thoughts to be expressed on paper, you can then resume your breathing exercises and allow yourself to experience peace of mind.

Notice how I asked you to experiment with this exercise for only five minutes? For many of you this may have been the longest period of time you've sat still without doing anything (other than sleeping, watching television) in a long while. By starting with five minutes of relaxation breathing each day and adding five minutes each day thereafter, you can build up to 20 to 30 minutes per day by the end of a week. Perhaps your goal is one hour per day—that's great. Just remember, this exercise is designed to relax you and get you in a peaceful state of mind; it isn't a competition to see how long you can meditate.

TIP When I first began meditating, I assisted my learning process by using certain meditation tapes and soft music to help me relax. This may be helpful for you as well. Concentrate on repeating the same word over and over or on rubbing a smooth stone, which can aide you in learning to relax.

Let the Process Unfold

Purpose never ends. It unfolds at the right time, in the right place, and continues on long after we are physically gone. Earlier, I mentioned Christopher Columbus and that his purpose still lives on. So does the purpose of Thomas Edison and that of millions of other individuals who have lived in purpose.

When you allow yourself to be, your purpose may shift many times in your life. Stay *unattached* to the actual destination and allow the process to unfold. Many people are confused by this approach to life because they are so invested in setting goals and arranging exactly how their lives will turn out. It may be a challenge to accept the concept of "do what you love and the money will follow." Often this sounds too good to be true and not tangible enough for our "doing" side to handle.

I had difficulty grasping this concept myself. I had followed my dream and not only did the money not follow—I went broke (temporarily). So when I began my career consulting practice, I incorporated some *practical* steps to discover my purpose along with the concept of following my heart and doing what I love. These steps have worked well for me and hundreds of others I've counseled over the years.

Practical Steps for Discovering Purpose

In *Getting Hired in the '90s*, I suggest an exercise on writing down your ideal career. This entails allowing yourself the freedom of no limitations, like a child filling out her Christmas wish list. Take out a piece of paper, give yourself an hour of uninterrupted time, and remove all limits. Ask yourself, "If I had all the money in the world, what would I do in my career?"

When I wrote out my ideal position, I had a difficult time getting past the concept of being able to be a writer without the experience or credentials. It seemed a bit far-fetched to me at the time. However, I allowed my intuition to guide me, and even though it didn't make logical sense, I persisted in affirming that it could really happen.

Once you have your ideal position in place (for those still having difficulty deciding on what you choose to pursue, it may be wise for you to invest in the assistance of a qualified career counselor), you can then create a map that will set you in the proper direction. In Chapter 4, we will discuss how to create a lifelong career plan to get you on track. We will also talk about how important engaging a "coach" will be to your success.

As you can see from my life's journey to finding my purpose, there were many ups and downs along the way. The biggest challenge I faced was staying motivated during that time. In addition to having several supportive friends, colleagues, and coaches, finding my life's purpose required me to be self-disciplined and self-motivated. So, how do you stay motivated when the bills are mounting, everyone seems to be against your project or purpose, and you can barely see the light at the end of the tunnel?

Staying Motivated along the Long and Winding Road

I think of life as a good book. The further you get into it, the more it begins to make sense.
Harold S. Kushner

I used to be one of those people who started projects enthusiastically only to discover that when the going got tough, my excitement waned. I gave up on more projects than I care to remember. At one time during my book writing, I did give up. However, this time things were different—because I was different and willing to do things differently. I actually made a conscious effort to learn how to stay motivated. Here are some of the actions I took:

TEN TIPS TO STAYING FOCUSED

1. I kept a daily journal of my actions. Whenever I would get down and think I wasn't far enough along, I would take out my journal and focus on how far I'd come instead of how far I had to go.
2. I took several three-by-five-inch cards and wrote my dream on each of them. I taped them to my mirror, my desk, even the visor of my car. When I asked myself why I was pursuing this crazy dream, I was reminded by these cards.
3. I listened to motivational tapes and read inspirational books. I surrounded myself with positive information and people who had met their goals, and I avoided negative news and people. In fact, I eliminated the television news from my life completely. I used this time instead for filling my mind and soul with gourmet food rather than junk food.
4. I visualized my dream several times each day. I playacted the positive results in my mind as though they were reality.
5. I shared my dream with only a handful of people who truly believed in me. I turned to them for support when I wasn't feeling optimistic. They helped remind me of why I was doing all this.
6. I focused on my spiritual side. Up to this point, I had never paid too much attention to faith in a higher source. I started to read books about faith; attended workshops; visited churches, temples, and so on, to connect with my higher power again.
7. I made agreements with myself and kept them. When I felt like going out instead of writing, I would negotiate with myself. If I wrote for one hour, I would reward myself by doing something special for myself.
8. I learned to ask others for help. Doing that was a stretch for me, but I realized that I couldn't write a book, run a business, and be a single mom all alone.
9. I volunteered my time and services. Not only did this make me feel good, I believe we get back 10 times more than we give.
10. I followed my plan, and I spent time preparing for things instead of winging them. When I got sidetracked, I had a plan to get back on course again.

My purpose is still unfolding. If you had asked me even two years ago where I'd be at the present time, I couldn't have predicted it. I have allowed my life to flow in the moment and have proceeded in areas that I never dreamed possible. When you begin to allow events to unfold at their own speed, you'll become aware of opportunities that you never saw before.

This isn't to say that you shouldn't have a strategy. It just means to allow some flexibility in your plan so that you can take advantage of opportunities that spring up along the way. In Chapter 4 we will take an in-depth look at developing your plan and living your purpose without necessarily leaving your job.

Checklist for Moving On

	Yes	No
1. Have you given up "trying"?	___	___
2. Have you committed to discovering purpose?	___	___
3. If you are in "limbo," have you taken steps to leave and recommit?	___	___
4. Have you looked at your protections and do you understand that you are in control of your emotions?	___	___
5. Have you given yourself a tune-up?	___	___
6. Did you practice the forgiveness exercise?	___	___
7. Have you allowed yourself to become quiet (or meditate) to hear your inner-voice?	___	___
8. Have you practiced "being" rather than "doing"?	___	___
9. Have you allowed the process to unfold?	___	___
10. Did you write out your ideal position?	___	___
11. Have you incorporated some form of ongoing motivation in your daily life?	___	___

► 4 ◄

Positioning for Your Future in the New World of Work

Where there is an open mind, there will always be a frontier.
Charles F. Ketterling

Change Is a Sign of the Times

Okay, so the '90s have been filled with tremendous ups and downs. What decade hasn't been? Maybe the "good old days" are long gone and two-income families are a must. Perhaps you'd prefer the simple life of the '50s or the high-income lifestyle of the '80s? A statement from *The New Work Habits for a Radically Changing World*, by Price Pritchett (Dallas: Pritchett & Associates, 1994), sums it all up: "You're not going to like some of this. Chances are, nobody will like it at *all*. But that is neither here nor there. Question is, will you get with the program anyhow?" Yesterday is gone and tomorrow isn't here yet. What's left? TODAY. This moment.

Perhaps you're saying, "But I am willing to accept the changes going on today." Maybe, maybe not. Read the following, and then ask yourself again.

The Most Willing Person on Earth

"I am the most willing person on earth." This is not entirely true. Let me rephrase that. "I am the most willing person on earth when it comes to doing something that I want to do." This is not entirely true either. Let me rephrase that as well. "I am the most willing person on earth when it comes to doing something I want to do and there are no obstacles in my path." Hold it! That is pretty close but not quite. Okay? Okay. "I am the most willing person on earth when it comes to doing something I want to do and there are no obstacles in my path as long as I don't have to expend too much effort." Wait a minute. That's not it. I've got it. "I am the most willing person on earth as long as I don't have to change." Anything. As long as I don't have to change anything, you can count on me to do whatever it takes.

Anonymous

One of the main ingredients of living a successful life and coping well with change, according to David McNally, author of *Even Eagles Need a Push* (New York: Delacorte Press, 1991), is to first *understand that pain is part of life and it serves a good purpose*. David says, "Experience, embrace and learn from pain, do not resist it—it will help you move through it and benefit from it more quickly."

What Do Employers Really Want?

**Since we cannot change reality,
let us change the eyes which see reality.**
Nikos Kazantzakis

Employers want you to act *like an owner*. Why is this? Organizations are breaking into smaller components, and there's less hierarchy. "The move is toward small, decentralized business units that operate more independently," according to Price Pritchett in his book on the new work habits. The days of entitlement are long gone! No longer can you rely on your tenure or past skills and experience to keep your job. *Owners* understand that they must earn their keep each and every day. *The world does not owe them anything.* Companies are reshaping themselves in an attempt to become more entrepreneurial; therefore, in order to position yourself for success in the *New World of Work*, so must you.

Twenty-Five Qualities You Must Possess
to Be Successful in Today's Marketplace

The following are qualities to help you think and behave like a successful owner (see the chapter in parentheses for more information):

1. Takes calculated risks (Chapter 4).
2. Feels fear but isn't stopped by it—lives in the moment (Chapter 2).
3. Takes responsibility for actions (intentions = results, Chapter 1).
4. Makes good decisions (Chapter 2).
5. Is versatile and acts swiftly (Chapter 13).
6. Makes commitments and agreements and keeps them (Chapter 3).
7. Perseveres—follows through on ideas (Chapter 3).
8. Is curious—asks the right questions and asks for help (Chapters 2 and 4).
9. Invests in lifelong learning (Chapter 7).
10. Focuses on solutions not problems—results oriented. Has highly developed conflict-resolutions skills (Chapter 4).
11. Adds value to company, community, and customer (Chapters 4 and 11).
12. Is an effective communicator (Chapter 6).
13. Is self-disciplined and motivated—proactive (Chapter 3).
14. Is well-informed (Chapter 5).
15. Networks effectively (Chapter 8).
16. Believes in a life purpose (Chapter 3).
17. Follows intuition (Chapter 3).
18. Has fun (Chapter 2).
19. Doesn't believe in entitlement—earns keep (Chapter 4).
20. Is nonjudgmental (Chapter 9).
21. Makes mistakes and learns from them (Chapters 2 and 4).
22. Is proactive not reactive. Manages emotions (Chapters 3 and 13).
23. Has upbeat attitude—caring, loving person—follows Golden Rule (Chapter 10).
24. Is a team player—collaborates—doesn't compete (Chapter 4).
25. Relies on faith to be guided through adversity (Chapter 10).

Learning How to Think and Act Like an Entrepreneur

What does being an entrepreneur entail? It means being one who launches or manages a business venture, often assuming risks. To risk you must be willing to suffer loss. However, *a smart entrepreneur takes calculated (based on information and experience) risks*.

As far back as I can recall, I was a risk taker. No, I wasn't born this way. I have learned to take risks. I have found that more often than not, when I take a knowledgeable risk, I get good results. *Are you a risk taker or do you play it safe?*

Although it is important to take a risk, an entrepreneur must follow up the risk by taking action. This is what separates the successful risk takers from the ones who fail. Often it takes many failures before one can truly become successful. We all know Babe Ruth held the record for the most home runs. A little-known fact, however, is that he also held the record for the most strikeouts. What makes a person willing to get up to the plate and risk putting his heart and soul into the game of life with the chances of striking out? Because the rewards of getting a hit or home run far outweigh the temporary results of striking out or never getting up to bat at all. Remember the saying "It is better to have loved and lost than never to have loved at all"? Do you believe that?

Avoiding risks means that you avoid living life. You are more of an observer than a participator. So how do you become a risk taker when you are accustomed to playing it safe? Follow the Ten Tiny Steps in Chapter 1 to expand your comfort zone. Start with a small risk, so that if it doesn't pan out, it won't cause you or others harm. As you begin to take these risks and see some positive results, you'll grow more confident in assuming larger risks. In addition to taking risks, owners focus on solutions—not problems.

Becoming Solution Oriented

When I began writing my first book, I assumed I would find a publisher. I had a problem! No publisher—no book, right? Wrong! Instead, I focused on several solutions to my problem. I had plans B, C, and D all ready to go. Because my *intention* was to get my message out to the public, and I wasn't attached to how that would happen, I was able to solve the problem by self-publishing the book.

When we are growing up, we have our parents and teachers to solve our problems for us. We soon realize, however, in the real world, we must learn to solve our own problems. Often we get caught in the trap of focusing on the problem rather than the solution.

Example: Due to constant interruptions (phone calls, employees wanting help, etc.), Karen found herself with a huge time-management problem. She fell behind in entering data (necessary for her to do a good job) into the computer in a timely manner. Karen was backed up for two weeks, was the only one in her company who knew how to use the software program, and was already working overtime. She felt overwhelmed, overworked, and defeated. Each day, she put off this task until it became such an enormous job that she could no longer see the light at the end of the tunnel. Before leaving each night, she promised herself, "Tomorrow I will begin this project." Tomorrow never came.

What solutions were possible for Karen? When I asked her this question, she informed me that she had tried them all, and the only solution was to wait until a "slow" period at work to catch up. I suggested she look at three different options:

1. Hire a temporary employee (with this particular software experience) to input the data. Have the temp train another employee at the same time.
2. Come in on a weekend (uninterrupted time) and input data. Cross-train another employee at the same time.
3. Block out two hours per day (no phone calls, etc.) to devote to the project.

Karen informed me that there was no budget to hire a temporary, so solution 1 was not an option. She also explained that she could not input the data during the workday because that would require that no one in the company use the system during those two hours. Karen selected option 2. She approached her comanager and offered to teach her this new software package in return for helping her with the input. This manager jumped at the chance to learn this system and agreed to come in on two consecutive Saturdays to get the job done.

The second part of this problem is how to maintain the data entry on a regular basis so it doesn't back up again. Karen now blocks out one hour each day (she gives the receptionist the names of clients she absolutely has to speak with), and feels a new control over and energy for her job. No longer does she have to face the awful feeling of being behind, and she also recognizes the importance of controlling her time and focusing on solutions.

Are you facing a particular problem right now that you are stuck in? Step out of yourself and your emotions for a moment. Ask yourself, "If I were to focus ONLY on the solutions, what would they be?" Or ask your advisory board (Chapter 5) to assist in devising several solutions—then take action! Remember, the only way to learn about solutions is to be willing to make mistakes and learn from them.

Why Mistakes Are Good and How to Learn from Them

I used to absolutely hate making mistakes. Seldom would I admit that I even made them. Somewhere along the line, I learned to believe mistakes were bad. When we judge mistakes as bad, we go to great lengths to avoid making them. I now feel very different about making mistakes. Mistakes are only problems when you make the same ones over and over again and *don't learn from them.*

Some of our greatest inventions have been due to mistakes. Take the Post-it note for example. According to hearsay, an engineer at the 3M company left some epoxy on his work space and a note stuck to it. He probably thought, "Hey, what if I could make a sticky substance that could attach to paper and at the same time, be removed easily." An idea was born.

When I decided to self-publish, I went in search of the least-expensive-price-per-copy printing company. After reviewing several quotes, I selected a firm and proceeded to determine how many copies I would have printed. Based on my sales to date, I projected I could sell 10,000 copies in a short period of time. The sales associate who worked at the printing company explained that although I would get a better per-copy price by purchasing 10,000 copies, I may want to go with 5,000 to begin with (at a higher per-copy price), just in case. I did not take her advice.

Although the books did sell eventually, the extra cost of insurance, warehousing, and the crimp in my cash flow almost put me out of business. This was a very costly mistake. Why didn't I listen to someone who had 20 years of experience in the business? Because I thought I knew better. Of course, I learned from this mistake, and for the next printing, I ordered only 5,000 copies. I also learned an important life lesson. *Look to other successful people in your industry or field and learn from their mistakes.* It's much less costly and painful!

Take some time to recall some of your business mistakes. What did you learn from them? What did you do well? What could you have done better? And how will you handle a similar situation the next time? Another important criterion for being successful in the *New World of Work* is to be an active team player who manages projects.

Playing on a Team and Learning to Be Project Oriented

"The old hierarchical way of management is no longer serving the information-based economy that we have become," according to Tom Troy, partner at Team Architects in Chicago. "As new types of companies emerge in this new economy, management and staff must develop new skills that fit the growing demand of managing projects rather than managing people."

The following are practical steps to becoming a better team player:

1. Examine your beliefs about being a part of a team.
2. Ask yourself, "What was my first experience of being on a team?"
3. Interview your team leader or other team leaders to see if your views on teamwork match.
4. Develop team communication skills. Tom Troy suggests, "Power struggles happen all the time on teams. Someone always has just a bit more authority than the rest of the group. When a situation occurs that engages you in a power struggle, your intuitive reaction may be to use authority to overpower them and get your way. Although this seems to solve the problem for you for the moment, the person you have overpowered may feel powerless and look for alternative ways to feel powerful. They will usually do this in a negative way. Rather than being locked into a power struggle, learn to negotiate a win-win situation over a win-lose situation."
5. Develop good conflict-resolution skills. In my many years of consulting and interactions with the corporate world, I've found most individuals avoid any type of conflict. They go to great lengths to steer clear of conflict and often find themselves embroiled in an even deeper negative situation. Most of us were

never taught conflict-resolution skills. Tom Troy suggests using a consistent form of communication to solve conflicts:

—"When you . . ."
—"I feel . . ."
—"What I want is . . ."
—"Will you do that . . ."

Tom also recommends that when negotiating a solution to the conflict, it is important to do so in a calm state of mind. Anger will sabotage your efforts at truly arriving at a win-win situation.

In addition to learning to take the necessary steps to become an effective team player, you may be challenged by the lack of individual recognition often associated with being a part of a team. In order to feel good about your contribution to the team and the company, you must stay visible in the group, and to key company decision makers. To ensure that this happens, you can define your relationship with the team leader and other team members. Explain that you require recognition for your individual efforts. Make sure you communicate this in a clear *nonthreatening* way. Get feedback from the leader and group to see if they have a clear understanding of what is important to you and that you will hold them accountable for their actions if you aren't getting acknowledged for your contributions.

The team attitude truly gives us all what we really want, whether we know it or not. What we *really want within a family, community, or organization is to feel valuable and powerful and to have a sense of belonging to the group.* Be willing to learn from your mistakes. Being in "team" fosters a great deal of self-awareness. You can learn a great deal about how to improve your skills both through this new awareness and the suggestions of team members and facilitators. Remember, find the good news in your mistakes and lighten up! Being part of a team is a lot of fun.

Now that you are somewhat familiar with the Twenty-five Qualities You Must Possess to Be Successful in Today's Marketplace and into the twenty-first century, you can incorporate them into a career plan to get you to the next level. First, however, you must determine if you are a "good fit" for your current job and how you arrived at where you are!

11/26/99

Evaluation: Are You a "Good Fit" CROWN RM AGENT
for Your Current Position?

	Yes	No
1. Do you enjoy your position at least 75% of the time?		✗
2. Do you believe in and support your company's mission statement?		✗
3. Do you have the skills and qualities that are required for your position?		✗
4. Do you have a good relationship with your manager and coworkers?		✗
5. Are you being well compensated for your work?		✗
6. Do you feel passionate about your work?		✗
7. Are you proud of your position and company?	✗	
8. Are you challenged by your job and learning new skills?		✗
9. Are you recognized and respected for your contributions?	✗	
10. Do you look forward to going to work?		✗
11. Are there opportunities for continued growth and challenge?	✗	
12. Does your position allow time for a personal life?	✗	
13. Are you having fun at work?		✗
14. Do you fit in well within your corporate culture?		✗
15. Do you believe your current position fulfills your purpose in life?		

If you answered NO to more than two of the above questions, you can choose to develop a plan to improve your current position. Often when there is something missing from a relationship (including your work relationships), we feel there is no alternative but to move on. We all know that the grass is not always greener on the other side. Before you leap to conclusions about leaving your position, let's examine ways to improve and enhance your current situation by learning from your past.

Understanding How You Got to Where You Are Now

Surveys indicate it is seldom salary that prompts an employee to look for a new position. Typically it is lack of recognition, which salary can reflect, and lack of feeling appreciated that prompt employees to leave an organization.

Before you can create a winning career plan, you must first understand where you are and how you got there. Take 30 minutes to stroll down memory lane. Think back to how you got your first job. Why were you excited about the opportunity? Were you just happy to get hired, or did you really want the opportunity? Did you prepare and plan to get it, or did you just happen upon it? Has your career just "happened to you," or have you directed it based on your interests and desires?

Like many of my high-school peers, I was like a ship without a rudder. I was more interested in socializing and getting out of school than I was in preparing for my future. This isn't always such a bad thing. Because I had little direction, I was willing to investigate anything in order to find out what to do when I grew up. I took most of my jobs because they were offered to me, rather than with any plan in mind. I drifted from company to company and job to job during the first few years of my career. Little did I know at the time that I was discovering *what I did not desire to do before deciding what I desired to do*.

I attempted to return to college during this time; however, I became discouraged because most of the courses I took were based more on theory than on real life. I was into experiencing real life and didn't believe I was getting what I needed from college. I began feeling like a misfit! It seemed as though many of my friends had gone on to college, were settled in their careers, and I was still going in circles.

When I accidentally learned about the recruiting industry, I felt like I had found my home. After all, I had been finding jobs for my friends and family for years. Now I could do what I was good at and get paid for it! Had I known about planning my career earlier, I could have avoided many of the pitfalls along the way. However, as I now know, I was on the "hard knocks" path in life and planning didn't interest me. If I would have taken the time to evaluate what I had interest in and what was available in the marketplace, perhaps I would have selected the recruitment field much earlier in my career. If I knew then what I know now, I would have been dangerous!

No matter where you are in your career, you can avoid many unpleasant experiences and enhance your success by looking at your past and learning from your experiences. Ask yourself the following: "What did I do right in my job selections? What could I have done to improve my choices?" Use this information while formulating your plan.

Creating a Winning Career Plan

Only a small percentage of individuals know at a young age what they desire to do the rest of their lives. Often they find their purpose early, for instance, due to an illness or death in the family that may prompt them to become, say, a doctor. Or perhaps they find a mentor or someone who recognizes their natural talents and encourages them to follow their heart's desire. For the rest of us, we either follow in the footsteps of our families because that is all we know or are encouraged to do, or we drift aimlessly in search of our dream.

> **I'll tell you a secret. Adults don't know what they want to do for a living. That's why they're always asking kids what they want to be when they grow up—they're looking for ideas.**
> *Paula Poundstone, comedian*

When I was in high school I loved to write. When I approached my English teacher about pursuing a career in her field, she discouraged me because of the lack of opportunities for growth. It didn't occur to her to focus on what I could do that might be related. I also had a strong interest in commercial art. I lived near a man who did this for a living and questioned him about a career in his industry. He was also discouraging and painted a gloomy picture of the future for commercial artists. So I did what all good girls of the '70s did: I learned to type. My mother always told me I could fall back on that skill if all else failed. I became a secretary.

Of course, now my typing skills have come in handy for typing my own manuscripts. Mom was right after all! More often than not, *parents play a huge role in deciding our careers.* Unfortunately, many times parents influence us based on their goals for us without taking into consideration what is best for us. Parents often feel that if the career they have chosen is good enough for them, why shouldn't their children choose it as well. Over the years, I have counseled hundreds of people who after attempting to fulfill their parents' dream realize they are miserable.

Take the case of Fred, for example. His father was an attorney as was his grandfather, and so on. Fred did not feel confident enough to face his father at a young age to let him know that he didn't want to follow in the family tradition. So he went to law school, earned his degree, and has been unhappily practicing law for years. Fred suffers from migraine headaches, has low self-esteem, and is an unhappy man. When I inquired what Fred would really like to do (if Dad weren't in the picture), he excitedly replied, "I would become a landscaper." Instead, Fred spends his days handling real estate closings and bankruptcy hearings. Can you relate to Fred's story?

The good news is that it is **never too late for a new career plan.** In fact, just recently a 65-year-old woman was interviewed on the news program *20/20* about her changing careers to become a flight attendant! She had always dreamed of becoming involved in the airlines, and after owning a hair salon for 30 years, she decided to pursue her dream. The wonderful news is that she is now employed with the airlines as a flight attendant. You may have believed that 65 years of age is too old to become a flight attendant; however, her own belief system created her reality. The following ten steps will help you customize your own career plan:

Career Plan Outline

1. Assess where you are at and how you got there.
2. Review the 25 qualities on page 61 and determine what you choose to improve on.
3. List your likes and dislikes.
4. Learn how to boost your value in the marketplace and take action.
5. Improve your current position.
6. Stay aware of what's happening around you. Remain flexible.
7. Always have an up-to-date resume on hand.
8. Read every chapter of *Success 2000* twice.
9. Engage the assistance of a business or career coach.
10. Have fun!

Not everyone will choose to leave his or her current position, but for those who do, we will cover how to change careers in Chapter 12.

Accepting, Enjoying, and Improving Where You Are Now

After you've determined whether you are a good fit for your current position, make a list of everything you enjoy about your current job and company. This will help you in deciding what you choose to do more of. Next, make a list of the responsibilities you don't enjoy. Of course, this will be used to help you determine what you desire to do less often. Then there's always your attitude about what you are doing that makes the difference. Read Charles Mallory's book, *Workhealing* (Marina del Rey, CA: DeVorss Publication, 1994), for greater insight into loving your work.

> **. . . There's a story about three workers breaking up rocks.**
> **When the first was asked what he was doing, he replied,**
> **"Making little ones out of the big ones." The second said,**
> **"Making a living." And the third, "Building a cathedral." While each**
> **of these answers was, of course, accurate, I hope to convince the reader**
> **that the third answer was "true"—that is, more faithful**
> **to our commonly shared potential of humanness.**
>
> *John Julian Ryan, theologian*

Remember Patti from Chapter 1 and her frustration? She was ready to quit her job, but by *focusing on the tasks she enjoyed doing, she was able to turn her position around.* In essence, Patti was able to enhance her value to her current company and boost her value in the marketplace.

Boosting Your Value in Your Company and the Marketplace

The first step in boosting your value to your current organization is to positively embrace the idea of the *New World of Work* and determine the qualities you choose to improve on. Refer again to the Twenty-five Qualities You Must Possess to Be Successful in Today's Marketplace.

Write down at least three qualities you choose to improve on. Use the Ten Tiny Steps from Chapter 1 to assist you in this process. For example, perhaps you'd like to improve on being self-motivated. By taking small steps, you may choose to take a course (see Chapter 7), enhance your internal image (see Chapter 6), or join an association to network (see Chapter 8).

Bringing Your Company More Revenue Than Your Annual Salary

Julie Marcus, human resource manager for McGaw, an intravenous drug company, is a prime example of how to boost one's value by taking a nonrevenue-producing position and turning it into one that not only pays one's salary but saves the company additional thousands yearly. Julie saved her firm over $250,000 in recruiting costs in one year! Not only did she document the savings, but she also used her tremendous results as a leveraging tool in her career. At this time, Julie is the only nonmanager in the entire corporation who receives an annual management bonus.

What's her secret? Julie takes the position of recruiter to a whole new level. She views the human resource function as a revenue-generating center rather than a cost center. To Julie, human resources needs to be considered a sales function instead of an administrative one. By assuming this attitude, not only has Julie saved her company a great deal of money, but she has also secured her position in an ever-changing industry.

When Julie came to McGaw four years ago, the firm was reactive in its hiring methods. Having been trained as a recruiter for a placement agency, Julie understood the value of assuming a more proactive approach to hiring. Over a two-year period, she set up a system that is today being followed by the corporate headquarters. Julie was able to accomplish several things with her proactive approach. She has incorporated all of the 25 qualities necessary to be successful in today's marketplace, and it's paid off in big dividends for her and McGaw. Julie was promoted, she received a salary increase, she gained more visibility for herself and her company (see Chapter 6), and she has become a respected team player in her organization. By incorporating these tactics and engaging the help of a career coach, Julie has also avoided the dreaded "downsizing" surge facing many of today's employees.

Engaging a Career Coach for Ultimate Success

Why do individuals wanting to get physically fit employ a personal trainer? Because they choose someone to instruct them on the proper ways to exercise, to keep them motivated when they don't feel like it, and to get results more quickly. The same applies for a career coach! Employing a career coach can give you the extra edge in today's marketplace. The best athletes in the world know what great coaches can do for their careers. Even Dennis Rodman admits that his former coach is one of the biggest reasons for his success!

Coaches, sometimes called "success coaches," are part mentor, part cheerleader, part counselor, and part spiritual adviser. They can charge from $150 to $500 per month, or if you have a service to offer, perhaps you can barter for their services. When you are interviewing a potential coach, it's imperative that you hire someone who believes in you. Look for individuals who have a proven track record and "walk their talk." Be specific about what you desire and make a decision to follow their advice.

The benefits you can derive from engaging a coach are tremendous. You can increase your focus and direction in life, lead a more balanced and fulfilling life, increase your sales and profits, get assistance on solving problems, increase productivity, and ease some of the challenges or adversity in life. With all the services a coach can offer, however, remember it takes two. A coach is your partner, but it takes your commitment and action in order to have a successful relationship and see the positive results that can help you to become indispensable to your company or industry and stay hired in the '90s and beyond.

Staying Hired in the '90s and into the Twenty-first Century

Neil Schermitzler, area manager in human resources for Amdahl Corporation, says, "Employees must become street-smart and recognize the writing on the wall before layoffs occur." Here are some signs to look for in your organization:

Ten Signs to Recognizing When Downsizing May Happen to You

1. What you "read between the lines" seems different from what you hear.
2. Office supply budget is cut (when you are told to use the pencil sharpener instead of purchasing new pencils).
3. Restrictions or elimination of travel and expense budgets.
4. New product development plans are cut.
5. The rumor mill is increasing its turnout.
6. Key decision makers tell you not to worry.
7. Increases in employee turnover.
8. Insiders sell their stock.
9. Management speaks vaguely about future plans.
10. People stop talking.

If you see some of these situations occurring in your organization, don't panic. Just stay aware. Keep an updated resume on file, and by all means read Chapter 12!

If you've done your homework, and you have incorporated many of the techniques from this chapter, you may now have increased your value enough to warrant an increase in salary. Keep in mind, however, that salary is only a portion of living a fulfilled career life, and judge it accordingly.

Strategies for Getting the Highest Salary Possible

It's important to know your worth in the marketplace before negotiating a raise. *Most people make the mistake of going into the salary meeting unprepared*, not waiting for the proper timing, and getting emotionally involved.

First, you may decide to put your feelers out by conducting informal surveys within your industry association. You can also contact headhunters in your field and get the "going rate" for someone with your credentials. (A word of warning: recruiters don't want to be used. If you agree to go on an interview solely for using the offer to get a counteroffer from your current employer, it may backfire on you. You might be able benefit in another way from this headhunter someday in the future, so don't burn your bridges. Besides, counteroffers are not good negotiating tools. Read why *never* to accept a counteroffer in *Getting Hired in the '90s.*)

When you have determined your value, write a summary of how you have contributed to the organization. Focus on the benefits you've offered and the money you've saved or earned your firm. Include how you've improved yourself (extra courses, getting publicity, etc.) and how that's helped your firm. Pretend you are going on an interview for your current job. How would you sell yourself? Practice your presentation before the meeting. Have a figure in mind of what kind of increase you are looking for; however, don't offer the amount to your employer. Wait to hear what your employer has to say before you reveal your bottom line.

Use industry information and any printed materials you can to back up your request for additional income. Don't allow your emotions to enter into the picture. Don't say, "I feel I deserve this." Feelings don't count in determining raises; the bottom line is do you pay for your salary and more? When Julie Marcus documented her actions that saved her company $250,000, she was able to provide tangible proof of her savings and how it more than paid for her annual income. Not only was she able to earn an increase in her salary, she negotiated a bonus on top of that!

If your company is not able to justify an actual salary increase, opt for stocks, a bonus, other perks, or a new title that might bump you up a salary grade or that you can use in the marketplace to receive a higher salary. Whatever you do, don't threaten to quit if you don't get what you are asking for. Should your company turn you down flat, and you are definitely underpaid, be sure to read Chapter 12 thoroughly.

Determining salary worth has always been a challenge, and as we enter the twenty-first century and it seems jobs are shifting from "tasks" to "projects," the question of salary becomes even trickier. It's important to learn how to play on a team and still retain your individuality and visibility. And now that you know all that is expected of you in this *New World of Work*, the following chapters will aid you in thriving during the coming years, rather than just surviving.

Checklist for Moving On

	Yes	No
1. Have you made a decision to be willing to do whatever it takes?	___	___
2. Have you taken steps to develop the 25 qualities necessary to be successful?	___	___
3. Have you taken small risks and are you thinking and behaving more like an entrepreneur?	___	___
4. Have you taken the "Are You a Good Fit?" evaluation?	___	___
5. Did you take a walk down memory lane to determine how you got to your current destination?	___	___
6. Did you make a list of the tasks you do and don't enjoy at your current job?	___	___
7. Have you written down three qualities you choose to improve on?	___	___

(continued)

Checklist (*continued*)

	Yes	No
8. Have you taken tiny steps to improve these qualities?	⎯	⎯
9. Did you take time to recognize any red flags regarding downsizing?	⎯	⎯
10. Have you done research to determine your value in the marketplace?	⎯	⎯
11. Did you update your resume, write your summary, and practice your presentation to get a salary increase?	⎯	⎯

▶ 5 ◀

Understanding the Marketplace

Tapping into the Information Age

Dont wait for your ship to come in; swim out to it.
Anonymous

There has been more information produced in the last 30 years than during the previous 5,000. The industrial age has given way to the information age. So, how do the successful people manage the incredible amounts of information we are deluged with on a daily basis? They learn how to tap into what is available and understand how to use it effectively.

Becoming Your Own Information Manager

I used to subscribe to at least 10 business magazines and periodicals. I'd make it a point to read them all. As my workload increased and my time became a precious commodity, I found much of the material I used to read piling up in the "to-be-read" file. Several months would pass and the pile would grow so overwhelming and outdated that I would end up tossing it out just so I wouldn't have a reminder of how far behind I'd become.

Realizing I was then missing out on some key information, I decided to implement a more effective way of streamlining the process of being in the know. First, I determined what I enjoyed reading and what information available was crucial to the success of my business. Next, I proceeded to ask my advisory board (which we will discuss later in this chapter) what periodicals and information they read on a monthly basis. I informed them of what information I had access to, and we decided to swap information on a regular basis. Not only did this cut down on my reading time, it also saved me hundreds of dollars in subscription fees. I also made it a point to ask clients and other people I met on a daily basis what they read and listened to for information, and what they found most useful. I received many great ideas, and I will share them with you throughout this chapter.

In order to become an effective information manager, I suggest you do the following:

1. Do the proper research to discover what information you need to help you prosper in your business.
2. Set aside a regular time each week to read, listen to, or otherwise plug into this information.
3. Take action on the ideas you've learned and share information with others.

How to Find Out What's Going On Out There

In our busy lives, we must look for the fastest and easiest way to access the information we need to keep up with current events that affect our business and lives. The following are just a few of the sources you can tap into.

The Internet

You don't have to guess anymore at what the hottest Web sites are. You can log on at www.100hot.com/ for a Web site (updated weekly) that lists the most frequently visited sites on the Web.

National Public Radio

An easy, informative, and entertaining way to listen to what's happening in the world, National Public Radio offers commentary on a variety of business and personal topics and trends. NPR also interviews authors and other individuals who are in the know.

Business Book Summaries

Executive Summaries uses a magazine-style format to provide written summaries on the top business books in circulation. *FastTrack* offers the best business books condensed on tape. Each month you receive two 30-minute versions, with author interviews of the hottest new business books available (a real time-saver for the busy professional).

Business Periodicals and Newpapers

Entrepreneur Magazine is one of the best sources for the small-business person. I've clipped more articles from this magazine than any other periodical. *Success Magazine* is not only inspiring but also filled with information for the individual who wants to learn about today's hot topics. *Forbes* keeps you up-to-date on the financial conditions of the marketplace as well as on who the movers and shakers are. *The Wall Street Journal* may be somewhat pricey to subscribe to on a daily basis, but you will find so much information packed in it that it's worth the investment. *USA Today* is a great national business paper to keep you in the know. *Wired* magazine is not just for techies; it can help you keep abreast of all the latest trends in computers and the information highway.

Local business magazines and newspapers are also valuable. Most major cities have a business magazine or newspaper that focuses on the local happenings. Chicago has *Crain's*, which is a fabulous source for business information. And of course there is your local daily paper, which can help to keep you up-to-date on your community news.

TIP Many of these magazines are available on-line as well. Be sure to install the fastest modem possible on your computer for the quickest transmission of data.

Clipping Services

In the past these services have been somewhat cost-prohibitive for the general consumer; however, new services that are very cost effective are cropping up each week on the Internet. Just tell them the industry or subject matter you're interested in, and they'll clip the articles and send them to you!

Newsletters

There are too many to mention here. Check with your local library for a national directory of newsletters and tap into those that fit your needs. Ask clients and coworkers for recommendations.

Trade Journals

Once again, there are so many available—check with your library for a comprehensive list or look in the *Encyclopedia of Associations* (Detroit: Gale Research, Inc., 1996) to get a listing of associations that put out newsletters or magazines that are of interest to you. (Make sure to go outside your industry and learn about all industries that may affect you. Look for those industries that closely tie into yours or may have a ripple effect on your industry three to six months down the road.)

The Library

I can't emphasize enough the importance of visiting your library at least monthly. Not only does it provide many of the sources you'll need, it has access to hundreds of different sources from sister libraries. Get friendly with your local reference librarians; they can guide you to the most up-to-date information available.

Other Sources

Tom Derkas, vice president of Blue Mountain Advertising, offers this suggestion when looking for hard-to-find information: "Telephone or write the company or industry you are interested in learning more about and ask their public-relations department to send you a media kit. Quite often the media kit will include a trade journal or other periodical which may offer you the information you need."

In addition, you'll want to keep your eyes on the television. CNBC has a terrific business show lineup; CNN is always on the cutting edge as well. I prefer these news stations to the regular local network news as I don't have to watch 20 minutes of crime and disaster to find out what's going on out there.

Developing an Advisory Board for Greater Success

Several years ago I heard a well-known CEO comment on his success. He attributed much of his incredible success to his board of directors and advisers. I thought to myself, "How I wish I had a board of directors to help me!" All of a sudden it hit me! I didn't have to wait until I got successful to get help; I could choose to get help first—that would assist me in living successfully.

The concept is similar to that of developing your own sales team, which you'll read about in Chapter 8. Before I began selecting individuals to become part of my advisory board, I first determined what I had to offer, what I needed improvement on, and where I needed to look to find the proper mix of people to meet these needs. I had a strong background in sales management, communication skills, networking, and employment issues. I had little or no exposure to manufacturing, technology, finance (accounting and investments), legal issues, diversity issues, team training, public relations, education, and other areas of the service sector (health, travel, etc.)

As in networking, developing an advisory board requires you to build relationships first. Otherwise, these individuals will feel used, and rightly so. Another issue in developing a board is determining what, if any, fees may be involved. There are times when I require just five minutes of a person's time to get an answer or opinion. There are also times when I require an hour or so, and for that I expect to pay individuals for their time as a consultant (and of course I expect to get paid as well if they use me as a consultant). Otherwise, my advisers and I have a barter agreement—we offer each other equal amounts of time and information.

In order to have a successful and effective board, you must have balance. When developing your board, you'll want to look for individuals with some of the following qualities:

▶ Has access to and has built relationships with "influencers" and decision makers.
▶ Is a person whom you respect and who respects you.
▶ Is willing to share information equally.
▶ Is fairly easy to reach and returns calls promptly.

Recently when I found myself struggling over an account I was working on, I telephoned one of my advisers who, I knew, had dealt with a similar issue. I quickly explained the dilemma I was faced with, and she was able to respond to my situation with several solutions. (A great benefit of advisers is that they are not emotionally involved in the situation and can oftentimes see things more clearly than you can at the moment.) I was then able to go back to my client with a new perspective, and we resolved the conflict easily. I also made it a point to give feedback to my adviser on how well the situation turned out. She was not only glad to help me but felt good about my taking her advice.

Another important component to building a successful advisory team is to understand each person's business (and make sure each person understands yours) and keep the team members in mind while you are receiving information. For example, I knew that one of my advisers was looking for additional information on the latest in the publishing field. Through my daily communications, I ran across an organization I thought might assist her in her quest. I contacted her and passed along this information from which she has since benefited immensely.

Tom Derkas of Blue Mountain recounts a great example of sharing information. He had recently heard from a friend that the Steel Recycling Institute was looking to enter the automotive industry. Several weeks later, he ran into the PR director of the institute at his local health club. They began a conversation and Tom mentioned what he had learned. She informed Tom that, yes, the Steel Recycling Institute was doing a promotion involving the automotive industry, but that they were having trouble getting a donation. Tom knew a person at Saturn and offered to put them in touch. It turned out that the individual at Saturn was not the decision maker but was able to put the institute in touch with the right person. Saturn ended up donating a car to the institute for its promotion. Now the Steel Recycling Institute turns to Tom as a consultant for advertising and promotions—all from shared information!

What makes Tom so successful in his collaborations is not only his willingness to share information but his asking the right questions. Tom asks open-ended questions when he meets new people, questions such as "What's been happening with you lately?" or "What new projects are you working on?"

How to Use What You've Learned to Your Advantage and to the Advantage of Others

A couple of years ago a good friend (and member of my advisory board) was traveling to Seattle and just happened to pick up a newspaper devoted to employment issues. Upon her return she phoned me to inquire if I'd heard of it. She suggested I contact them regarding writing some employment articles, which I did. Not only did the newspaper run several of my articles, I picked up several lucrative consulting assignments as a result. When my schedule became too hectic to write for a local paper, instead of just telling them I was no longer interested in writing for them, I recommended the same woman who had referred the Seattle paper to me. They hired her, and she was able to add to her writing credentials.

Sharing information is vital to "staying in the know." Take at least one hour per week to take notes and gather information; then telephone or write to share it with others. The old saying "Whatever you give away comes back one hundredfold" is certainly true.

Dan Garms, CEO of The Garms Group, a high-tech executive recruiting firm in Barrington, Illinois, uses this philosophy: "When you succeed, we succeed." Dan has built his successful recruitment practice by readily sharing information with everyone he comes in contact with. "Never leave someone without thanking them and showing appreciation for their time and use of their intellectual property (information is power)." Because Dan practices daily what he preaches, not only has he excelled in the highly competitive world of recruiting for over 18 years, he never has to advertise for business—all his business comes to him through referrals.

Referrals are very valuable. I remember once assisting a career counseling client with learning the art of networking. Although we had ended our "paying sessions" and were just staying in contact, I still offered her some free advice, which she was most grateful for. She followed my suggestions and was quite successful at networking. She called me to pass along the name of someone she felt I ought to know. I telephoned this new contact and discovered how much we had in common. I was able to give this contact several business leads and ended up hiring her to help organize several projects I was working on! Creating win-win scenarios is all a part of sharing information.

Tom Derkas suggests to always "look to the future instead of pushing today. Don't look for the immediate rewards," he cautions, "rather look for the long term connection." When Tom read about a new Sprint Telecommunications office opening up in his area, he met with one of their new employees and learned they were looking to hire a legal firm. Tom went to work. He called a friend of his who was a partner at a law firm, and it turned out that although it had managed several telecommunication companies, the firm wasn't on the bidding list for Sprint. Tom hooked them up, and the firm won a large new account. Of course now Tom's company handles all the advertising and marketing promotions (along with printing jobs) for this law firm. As you can see, sharing information pays big dividends.

Keeping Pace and Moving Ahead by Collaborating Rather Than Competing

To collaborate means to work with others or to cooperate with an enemy who has invaded one's country. To compete means to vie with another. Collaboration promotes win-win circumstances; competing promotes win-lose situations. Another term destined to grow in popularity, credited to Ray Noorda, founder of Novell, Inc., is "co-opetition."

When I joined the ever-growing world of speakers and consultants, I was naive to believe we were all part of one big happy family. Instead what I found was that many of the consultants I spoke with were extremely protective of their contacts and knowledge and had no intention of sharing the pie with me! I attempted to convince these people how wonderful it would be if we were all able to share the pie and that there truly was enough to go around. It fell on deaf ears. Rather than spend all my time reeducating the "old school of thinking" consultants, I chose to work with new-thinking individuals who had a like-minded philosophy of collaborating.

Take George for example. He runs a firm that is involved in career marketing. Although at first glance we could be construed as competitors (after all, we do offer some similar services), we also each offered several services that the other did not. We decided to develop a strategic alliance that has worked well for over two years. This collaboration has resulted in many thousands of dollars in exchanged business—new business that neither one of us would have achieved on our own.

Recently I had the pleasure of collaborating with a firm that specializes in a specific area of management training that I was interested in. I chose not to diversify my business into including this segment of training, but I did decide to add this firm to my growing list of consultants I recommend to my existing clients. In turn, the firm offers me the same privilege. This collaboration works well for two reasons: first, because we respect and trust one another; second, because neither of us plans on diversifying into the other's specialization.

When I was in recruiting, I also collaborated with other recruiters. Although recruiting is known as a highly competitive industry, I found that by networking and developing strategic alliances with recruiters of different industries, we were all able to benefit immensely.

Many corporations are set up for both external and internal competition. As a result, we have adopted a severe case of "withholding information"—from other managers, other districts and regions, and so on. In order to be well-rounded, successful businesspeople, we must learn to share information rather than greedily hold onto it. *Collaboration requires the ability to risk.* When I share information or leads with other consultants, I often take the risk of losing a client. However, if I am confident in my abilities and my relationship with that client, I know I am taking a calculated risk rather than a foolish one.

The smart companies already know this philosophy and are using it. When Gae Veit, owner of Shingobee Builders, Inc., was asked to bid on an $8 million hotel project, she was both thrilled and a bit intimidated. She had deliberately avoided going after this big project because she felt her company was too small to be an effective competitor. Someone suggested she consider teaming up with a larger firm. That turned out to be excellent advice. Shingobee partnered with a larger builder and, as a result of that partnership, has gone on to build a new $17 million convention center—on its own! Another major partnership was launched in 1995 when the largest minority-controlled Pepsi-Cola franchise selected NationsBank as the lead bank to join with four minority-controlled banks to refinance a $33 million loan.

"Partnering involves teamwork and sharing resources. Successful partnerships ensure mutual success for the partners and our customers," says Paul Allaire, chairman and CEO of Xerox Corporation. The key words here are *sharing resources*. When is the last time you viewed your competitors in a new light? Ask yourself now, "In what ways can I look to create strategic partnerships, alliances, and collaborations with my clients, suppliers, and competitors? Create a meeting with coworkers—or if you are a business owner, your competitors or clients—and brainstorm ways in which you can work together to create win-win situations for all concerned. Collaboration, partnering, and strategic alliances are crucial components to enhance your success into the twenty-first century!

Checklist for Moving On

	Yes	No
1. Have you conducted the proper research to become an effective information manager?	___	___
2. Have you set aside at least one hour per week to read, listen, or tap into the computer?	___	___
3. Have you selected at least one new source to add to your list of current sources?	___	___
4. Did you begin the process of identifying and selecting your advisory board?	___	___
5. Have you taken action on sharing information with others?	___	___
6. Did you take the step of looking at your competitors as collaborators?	___	___
7. Have you taken action on developing strategic alliances?	___	___

▶ 6 ◀

Leveraging Your Career

Public Relations Strategies to Build Your Image

**I've seen a lot of guys who are smarter than I am
and a lot who know more about cars. And yet I've lost them
in the smoke. Why? Because I'm tough? No. . . . You've got to know
how to talk to them, plain and simple.**
Lee Iacocca

Public relations is one of the most misunderstood tools of business. Quite often we think of public relations as relating mainly to top level executives or people in the entertainment field requiring media attention to assist them in building their careers. In this chapter, you'll learn why public relations can be important in managing your career and how to be your own PR agent.

First, let's explore why public relations can be crucial to enhancing your career. According to Anita Brick, owner of the Encouragement Institute in Chicago, "P.R. is professional visibility—to be known as an expert in your field and to be seen by your target audience of prospective employers and clients."

Years ago it seemed to be enough to work hard and have your work noticed. With all the changes of reorganization, reengineering, and downsizing, *many individuals whose work is exemplary are falling between the corporate cracks simply because their voice is not being heard by the decision makers*. With many firms relying on team efforts, often the leader of the team is given credit (or takes credit) for the ideas of the entire team, and therefore your specific efforts may go unrecognized by the "influencers" in your company or industry. When it comes time for cutbacks or "rightsizing," only the most visible team members will keep their jobs. Let's face it, the number of jobs available is decreasing every day. Because of this extremely competitive culture, fear of losing one's job may cause a normally ethical person to sabotage another's ideas or take them on as his or her own.

To prevent these situations from happening and taking you by surprise, *I suggest you assume a more proactive role in managing your career* by implementing a public relations plan to insure your professional visibility, both internally and externally. Let's begin where your influence is greatest, your current company.

Internal Public Relations and Image Building

Most of us have been taught that humility is an admirable quality. We've learned to look upon those who toot their own horn as egotists, braggarts, and the like. We have also learned to downplay our special qualities and to minimize our talents and uniqueness. In order to be effective in developing a solid public relations plan, you must first learn to understand the difference between bragging and knowing why you are a good deal.

Take a look around you and study those people who are currently enjoying success. What must they believe about themselves? If you met Michael Jordan and told him what a superior basketball player he was, how would you respond if he replied, "Oh, I'm not really that good, I'm just lucky"? Would you believe him? No! You'd probably think to yourself, "Oh sure, he's got to know how good he is." Would you be offended if he replied, "Why, thank you. I've put a great deal of energy into my success, and it's good to know that you appreciate me"? Wouldn't you feel he was being more sincere if he truly acknowledged his talent? *Good public-relations strategies start with acknowledging your talents.* Take some time now to write down three qualities that you like or admire about yourself:

1. _____ .
2. _____ .
3. _____ .

Look at your list and notice how it feels to give yourself credit for these talents or qualities. Keep at it until you start to feel comfortable with acknowledging them. Once you can start admitting that you are a pretty good deal, you can then learn to accept and actually *celebrate yourself*.

You grow up the day you have your first real laugh—at yourself.
Edith Barrymore

Long before he became champion of the boxing world, a young fighter by the name of Muhammad Ali spoke four words that were heard around the globe: "I am the greatest." Many people were offended by his statement, others amused. Now, did Muhammad actually believe he was the greatest? Probably not when he first began; although by repeating these four words over and over, not only did he eventually believe them, but these words became a reality. *What is your reality?* Take a few moments to write a statement that celebrates your specialness. (Even if you don't quite believe it yet, write it down anyway.) Repeat this statement daily—look in the mirror and say it; say it while you're driving or taking a shower; keep repeating it until it becomes your reality.

When I was writing my first book, I used this exercise daily. I repeatedly told myself that I was a published author! What would have happened if I had told myself, "Oh, you'll never get published. Who do you think you're kidding?" Our thoughts create our reality, so as the old saying goes, fake it till you make it!

Jim Carrey told this story when interviewed by Barbara Walters for ABC's *20/20*: Day after day, year after year, this struggling actor dragged himself out to Mulholland Drive in California, looked out over the mountains, and told himself that he was a successful actor and that agents were clamoring to sign him up. He went so far as to write himself a check for $10 million. Well, you know the rest. Jim Carrey received over $10 million to appear in *Mask II*. **Remember, you are your own hardest sale—once you buy yourself, others will be sold on you as well.**

After you've developed your statement, *share it with others*. If you are experiencing difficulty uncovering your unique talents, ask others who know you well to assist you. Request that they tell you three qualities they admire in you. *Listen carefully* to what they tell you and trust that they are being truthful. Use these qualities in your statement.

Practice these new beliefs each and every day. When someone gives you a compliment, and you are about to shrug and say, "It's nothing," respond instead by saying, "Thank you." Eventually you might even add, "Thanks. I feel good about _____ , too!"

What most people don't realize is that when you refuse a compliment, basically you are telling the other person that he or she is wrong. For example, when your boss tells you how much she appreciated your promptness on the project you just completed, and you respond by saying, "Well, I could have done better if I only had more time," you are telling your boss that she was mistaken about how good you are; and not only will she discontinue her compliments, but she will eventually begin to believe your low opinion of yourself.

When you learn to respond to your bosses (or other individuals) by using positive comments about yourself, you'll start to notice different results. So, the next time you receive an acknowledgement for a job well done, respond by saying, "Thank you for noticing. You are right, I did my best on this project, and I appreciate your support." **Remember, we train others how to treat us.** Once we become comfortable accepting others' praise, we can learn to promote ourselves.

This process takes time and practice. If you are like many people, you've spent years denying your uniqueness, and in order to assume new behaviors, you must be committed to doing things a new way. Remember, *if you keep doing what you are doing, you'll keep getting what you are getting. So if you don't like what you are getting, you can choose to change what you are doing.*

Acknowledging Others

As you are learning to acknowledge yourself, you must also learn to acknowledge others. Unfortunately, many people think of this as "kissing up" or brown nosing, but it isn't unless your compliments are not sincere. When you respond with honest appreciation of others' talents and achievements, you won't be negatively labeled. Instead, you'll find that *the more compliments you give out, the more you'll receive.* However, choose your acknowledgments carefully. Overused compliments will cause others to be suspicious. Keep your acknowledgments focused on the person's abilities and use direct eye contact in your delivery.

Begin by giving credit or acknowledgment to individuals in your organization who are generally overlooked. Don't reserve your compliments for only those people you perceive as influential. Avoid shallow compliments and look for ways to make people feel special. The more you help people feel special, the more you'll be noticed by others. Use names often in conversation. The next time your assistant performs a task well, say something like, "I noticed how you anticipated my needs by bringing the Sterling account file to me when Ms. Sterling was on the telephone. I appreciate your attention to this, [insert name]. Keep up the good work!" Not only will you feel good about yourself by acknowledging others, but you'll help them feel good about themselves and you as well. *Employees and coworkers who feel good will be more productive and fun to work with.*

Keep in mind, however, that not everyone should be acknowledged in the presence of others. Gauge individuals' reactions to your compliments and use your discretion. Occasionally calling someone aside for acknowledgement shows that you aren't grandstanding, and it also avoids causing other employees who would have been within earshot to feel left out. Often, we only call others aside to tell them something they did wrong. If you *balance* your constructive criticisms with compliments, your coworkers and employees will not learn to fear your request to "see them for a moment."

The most effective management (and relationship-building) principle I've used in dealing with others was introduced by Dale Carnegie in his book *How to Win Friends and Influence People* (revised edition; New York: Pocket Books, 1982). He suggests using the "sandwich" approach when dealing with others regarding improvements or mistakes. *Start with a positive statement about the person. In the middle deliver the correcting statement, and follow that with another positive one.* By utilizing this simple approach you'll see amazing results!

Recall an experience or situation when your boss or coworker didn't use the sandwich approach. What if it went something like this? In frustration your boss tells you, "You didn't follow directions, and now we are behind schedule. You will have to do it again, so plan on staying late tonight. Now don't disappoint me again. See that I get this on my desk first thing tomorrow and it better be right!" How would you feel?

Would you feel differently if he had responded like this: "Jack, you are a valued employee to me, and your work on this project has been excellent to this point. I've noticed that there was a misunderstanding on my directions regarding this report. Please tell me what your understanding of my directions was? I want you to know how much we need your expertise on this project. How do you propose we get this rectified by tomorrow morning?"

Notice the difference words can make! When bosses or coworkers attempt to take away our power, we feel hurt, angry, and resentful. However, when we allow others to maintain their power, feel good about themselves, and learn from their mistakes (rather than fearing them), we will begin to see cooperation from others.

TIP Omit the word *but* from your vocabulary—replace it with *and.*

People will live up to the expectations you have for them. If you feel your coworkers and employees will continually let you down, they will. On the other hand, if you believe that mistakes are okay as long as we learn from them, and *you treat others as you would like to be treated,* you can make a terrific public relations agent for yourself and others! Now that you have a clear understanding of how important your attitude is in developing an internal public-relations strategy, you can create a plan to gain more visibility within your organization.

Getting Involved

Once you've laid a strong foundation within your company, close circle of friends, and business associates, you can branch out to other arenas. Start by identifying the talents you have to offer in your field of expertise and then choose new areas to use these talents. If you have good writing skills, offer to submit articles or conduct interviews for your firm's newsletter. Perhaps you are more inclined to be a good organizer; volunteer to assist putting together your company's annual convention or picnic. Whatever you choose, remember to find something you truly enjoy doing and do it willingly, not just to "score points." Regardless of what you decide to get involved with to become visible in your industry or company, learning to speak comfortably in front of a group is a necessity! The basic skills for successful public speaking are communication skills. Let's explore how important it is to be an effective communicator both in groups and one-on-one.

Communication Skills They Never Taught You in School

"I am thinking of a brown dog," I say. How would you respond to this? Most individuals reply as follows: "A German shepherd, a Doberman . . ." In other words, they make an attempt to guess what I am thinking. "Wrong," I say. "I was thinking of a dachshund."

Next I ask, "How did you feel when I told you that you were wrong?" "I don't know," they say. "Kind of bad, a little stupid." I then say, "What could I have said to you if it were important to me that you knew what I was thinking?" "Well, you could have told me it was a small dog," they suggest. "Or," I respond, "I could have said a dog shaped like a hotdog, right?" "Yes, that's right," they nod. Then I ask them, "What could you have done differently if you were interested in understanding what I was thinking?" "I could have asked you some questions, like does the dog have short or long hair, is it big or small, et cetera," they admit. "So, why didn't you?" I inquire. "I guess because I didn't think of it," they respond.

This is a classic example of how ineffective our communications skills are. By not giving others enough information and making them guess at the meaning of our statements, we help them misunderstand. *The responsibility for effective communication lies with both parties.* When others do not give us enough information to make an educated decision, we must ask questions to understand what they meant.

Now take the same example and see how effective communication works: "I'm thinking of a brown dog. What am I thinking of?" I say. You say, "Oh, what kind of dog are you thinking of?" I reply, "I am thinking of a dachshund." See how simple it is?

What makes us assume that others will know what we are thinking? One thing might be our life experience. If I had a brown dachshund while growing up, I might automatically assume that people would know what I was referring to. The other person may have had a Doberman and might equate that dog with the color brown. *When practicing effective communication skills, we must never assume that the party we are speaking to has had the same life experiences or has the same perceptions of the world as we do.*

Another form of communication that gets us into trouble is using the word *but*. For example, we start a conversation by saying, "I like the way you handled this project, *but* I wish you would have listened to my directions and done it this way." What do you think the other party hears? Only that you wanted it handled differently. They probably didn't hear that you gave them a compliment as well. Instead of using the word *but* in your conversations (which eliminates the sentence preceding the *but*), use the word *and*.

I was taught early in my sales career to choose my words carefully, as though I were choosing a golf club for the best shot. If you desire to make a putt, you won't choose a driver. The same applies to conversation. Think about what you desire to communicate, and once you have made your statement, ask questions to make sure the other party understands your intended meaning.

By using these basic communication skills, you will not only become an effective communicator, you'll see some great results! In addition to using these basic skills, I highly recommend subscribing to the terrific newsletter *Communication Briefings* (1-800-888-2084). It is a wonderful source for innovative and solution-oriented communication tips. Of course, all these tools will help you with your public speaking skills as well.

Gaining Exposure by Public Speaking

In the past, one of my greatest fears was getting up in front of a group and speaking. If you feel terrified of public speaking, you are in good company. I recall a particular event at which I received an award for my accomplishments in the recruiting industry. Over 600 employees were in attendance, and I was to accept the award and make a short speech. I actually became physically ill and couldn't eat the delicious dinner before the awards ceremony. Although I seldom drink alcohol, I did that evening, hoping to bolster my sagging confidence. When my name was finally called to go center stage and accept my recognition, I literally begged the master of ceremonies (our national training director) not to make me speak. He insisted I say a few words. I finally managed to blurt something out (although to this day I can't recall what I said), and what should have been a moment to celebrate my talents and shine among my peers instead left them wondering, "Who was she?"

Later in the evening I was approached by a young rising star in our company who offered this innocent comment: "I was so looking forward to hearing from you tonight—I've admired your work a lot and was disappointed that you didn't share some of your experiences with us." I was quite taken aback by her honesty and explained how uncomfortable I was with all the attention. I was surprised by her admission that she felt I had something of real importance to say. She looked at me quizzically, and her face reflected what I felt about myself. I really didn't deserve the award. I had nothing special to share. In the safety of my hotel bedroom that night, I cried. I felt as though I had let everyone down, mostly myself! By not believing in myself and succumbing to my fears, I had missed a tremendous opportunity to be visible to my peers and other influences. You see, *being visible means taking a risk to share part of yourself with others.*

When people hear me speak today in front of hundreds of people, they assume I am, and have always been, a naturally gifted speaker. Even when I explain that it hasn't always been that way, many don't believe me. When I assumed the belief that I had something special to share with others, I was able to channel my fear into enthusiasm. I practiced and practiced and practiced my message until I knew it in my sleep. I started speaking in front of a handful of people and worked my way up to bigger groups. I still get nervous before I speak. However, now I direct my nervous energy back into my speech, and it comes out as enthusiasm and excitement. Discover a special message (or talents) you have to share with your company, industry, or organization—start small and get out there and make yourself visible!

I guarantee you will receive more pleasure than pain. The feedback I get from others, along with knowing that I overcame many obstacles, helps me to feel proud of myself. Once you've mastered your craft or talent, *it's important to share it with others, so they can benefit from your experiences.* Volunteer to speak at corporate events, training sessions, conventions, and the like. Take a public-speaking course and practice your skill. If you choose to be a leader in your profession, you cannot afford to pass up the opportunities to speak in public.

When you meet the challenges of delivering your message (and becoming more visible) internally, you are ready to take it outside your firm. If you are still too petrified to take action on speaking in front of others, please remember where I began and know that it's alright to be terrified. *Know that I am no different from you, that I have just been doing it longer!* In order to gain the attention to attract speaking engagements, you must first create a press release to inform others of what you're about.

Developing a Press Release/Bio to Showcase Your Talents and Experience

If you aren't familiar with what a press release is, don't feel bad. At one time, neither did I. A press release/bio is a resume directed toward the media. I suggest you engage the assistance of an expert to compose one that is professional and truly reflects you and your talents. I attempted several times to write my own (after all, of all people, I should have known how to write, right? Wrong!); I failed miserably. I couldn't get out of my own way long enough to write objectively. Fortunately, you can hire, for a modest fee, a talented writer to put together a basic release, and you can polish it up yourself. After you've developed a basic press release/bio, you can customize it as you add new skills or experience to your repertoire.

Submitting Press Releases to the Proper Channels

Now that you've invested the time, money, and effort into developing a press release, don't let it sit in your desk drawer! Start by submitting it to your human resource department and letting them know you are available for interviews or to offer training. Depending on the size of your firm, you can also send it to your communications department, training department, and so on. I also suggest you send a copy to key decision makers. Be sure to inform your current boss of your actions to alert him or her to your activities. *Many companies require that press releases get the approval of the legal department as well, especially those for external use.*

Submit these releases often and regularly in order to get the best results. Submission timing is important. Look for timely issues that address your particular skill set. For example, your company has just announced that they plan to install a new computer network, and you have assisted another firm in a similar transition. Prepare a release geared toward this issue. Or perhaps you have taken a course on the Internet, and you have learned how to tap into a wealth of information that may help your company. Write an article to instruct your coworkers on how to overcome their frustrations and fear of the Internet and share simple steps they can take to help make their job easier. Simultaneously write a press release about what information you have to share and submit this to the editor of your company's newsletter. Remember to copy your human resource department and other key decision makers in your firm. Offer them personalized instruction and/or details as to how this information can be of value to the company.

Getting Noticed by Newsletters

Many firms have wonderful company newsletters. If your company doesn't have one, either make the request to get one started or, better yet, do it yourself! Easy-to-use software packages are now available to assist you. Becoming involved with the newsletter can increase your visibility in several ways:

1. The opportunity to write an article that will showcase your writing talent and position/industry experience.
2. The opportunity to have someone else write an article highlighting you and your accomplishments.
3. The opportunity to interview other influencers, and learn from them, network with them, and develop friendly, productive relationships with them.

Perhaps you work in or own a small company and do not have enough staff to warrant a newsletter. Participate in or start an industrywide newsletter—either way, you can't lose.

Appearing in Company Videos, Commercials, and Training Films

Tailor your press release to offer your expertise on video. If you've been in front of a camera before, send a copy of the tape along with your release. Offer your services to be used in any of your company's video productions. If you haven't been filmed before, take a course on how to present yourself professionally on film. If you photograph well, invest in having a professional picture taken and offer it for use in brochures or annual reports.

Be sure to keep your eyes and ears open for new projects to get involved in. Don't limit yourself to just your department. Learn who the key decision makers are in your company and develop relationships with them. Use e-mail, the telephone, or fax to stay in touch with these individuals. By using the relationship-building skills discussed in Chapter 8, you can build your own internal sales team to help promote your talents within your organization.

If you are contacted to work on a project or to be interviewed and you are not an appropriate source, decline the opportunity. Don't try to bluff your way through it; you'll only do yourself and your company a disservice. Instead, find someone who fits the bill more closely and recommend that individual. Ask to be kept in mind for a future project or to be contacted as a source to recommend others.

Becoming visible within your company and industry is a fun and rewarding way to meet new people, continue learning, gain recognition for your accomplishments, and share your message with others. It can also increase your confidence and income. *People who are visible earn more money than those who are not.* The proper kind of professional visibility will help you earn the credibility and respect you may feel you are not currently getting. In addition, strong internal public relations will ultimately lead you to opportunities outside your company and industry if you so choose. Think of it as an insurance policy for your career. If your company should reorganize or downsize next week, or even next year, will you be remembered?

External Publicity
(How to Engage the Media to Enhance Your Career)

If you are looking for the Andy Warhol fifteen minutes of fame, this section is not for you! Delving into the world of the media is not for everyone. Especially not the fainthearted. My first few attempts at getting media coverage (on a scale from 1 to 10) were about a 3. I contacted a major syndicated columnist who wrote about career issues. She hung up on me—twice! I soon realized that not everyone was excited to hear my story. I must admit that getting such a rude reaction took the wind out of my sails temporarily. However, as in sailing, when the winds act up, you can choose to adjust your sails. So I did.

Rather than take this situation personally, I chose another route. I selected another top columnist who also wrote about careers, and I called her. I asked her to do a review of my book in her column. She promptly informed me that she was under a deadline and had no time for me. Four phone calls later, the answer was the same. (I never said that I was a quick learner but that I've learned from the school of hard knocks—very hard knocks!) When I finally came to my senses, I asked myself what I was doing wrong. Why was I getting the same results? I knew that it was a cold, cruel world out there, but weren't there any nice people left? After feeling sorry for myself for a few weeks, I decided that I was being extremely self-centered and that I should put myself in the other person's position for a minute.

With this new awareness, I decided to recontact this columnist. However, I made sure that this phone call was different from the start. I got her attention by asking her some questions. She informed me that her husband was very ill and this was a bad time. I now understood that her abrupt tone during the first four calls was not directed toward me. I extended my condolences and suggested I could call back at a later, more convenient date. I then took out a note card and wrote her a fairly lengthy note. I explained that I could empathize with her situation because my mom was extremely ill also. I included a little something to cheer her up and told her I would call in a few weeks. That call turned the tables on our relationship. She greeted me very warmly, expressed her concern for my mom, and thanked me for my kind words. Without any prompting, she offered to write a column about my book and me entitled "Enlightened Perseverance." I laughed along with her and agreed that, yes, I was very tenacious and that was precisely the message I wanted to get across to job seekers everywhere—**DON'T EVER GIVE UP!**

Several weeks later, the column ran in over 100 papers nationwide, and within days, I had received over 1,000 orders for my book! But our relationship didn't end there. I decided I could learn a great deal from this experienced woman, and I wanted to cultivate a long-standing business relationship/friendship. Shortly thereafter, I was able to reciprocate by writing a column regarding her new book. I also gave her a few referrals that I had collected over the past several months. Not only was she extremely appreciative, but she also referred me to a writer from *Glamour* magazine who was looking for a quote. It's been over three years now since that first phone call. Not only has this woman been a tremendous inspiration to me, but she has also given me a written endorsement to use on the book cover for the second edition of *Getting Hired in the '90s*, has been my mentor, friend, and an ongoing source of helpful career experience and knowledge.

As you can see, even in the dog-eat-dog world of media, building relationships is key! I recommend you start small. Most universities have school magazines that are interested in alumni activities. Always read the magazine, newspaper, or periodical you are interested in appearing in before you call the editor. An editor's biggest gripe is that people don't take the time to do their homework and instead ask dumb questions that editors don't have time for.

Next, submit your release to your community newspaper. Again look for timely issues to tie in your field of expertise. Get to know the editors in your local community first. Ask what their current needs are on building relationships with others (refer to Chapter 8 on networking). Once you determine their requirements, you can submit your release, refer others, or send them articles that may be of interest to them.

After you've had some success at the local level, make copies of all articles you've appeared in. Be sure to send these articles to key influencers in your company to alert them to what you are up to. Begin building a portfolio of articles you can send to other editors to establish a track record.

Once you have established a local presence, you can move on to the national level if you choose. It's important to understand and use publicity to your advantage. Be sure to spend your time wisely. Research different publications and types of media that suit your talents and promote you successfully. Learn to leverage what you've done and use it to get other opportunities for visibility.

Getting More Visibility Than You Ever Dreamed Of!

After many tries at getting a review in a major women's magazine, I was finally successful in landing a small blurb and an excerpt from *Getting Hired in the '90s*. I could barely wait to get to the newsstand to purchase a copy. I must have read through the magazine three times before I spotted the tiny reference to my book. If I had such a hard time finding it and I knew it was there, I could imagine what the other readers' chances of seeing it were. So I did what any inspired self-promoter would do. I wrote a letter to the editor of the magazine, and instead of complaining (which was my first thought—after all I had given them an hour interview for five lines!), I thanked her for running the piece about my book and offered her readers a discounted price if they said they saw the offer in her magazine. What I discovered was that people really do read the "Letters to the Editor" section. I received over 300 orders from that letter alone. The old saying "When life gives you lemons, make lemonade" truly applies here.

Industry Trade Journals

When deciding on an external public-relations strategy, consider your industry's trade journals as a viable format for exposure. Not only can this kind of publicity get you visibility in your industry, but it can be a boost to your company's visibility as well. This kind of visibility comes in handy when it's time for a raise (your boss has tangible proof of your value) or when you are caught up in a lay-off (the article might interest other companies in your industry requiring your expertise).

Julie Marcus of McGaw Pharmaceutical is a great example of leveraging her publicity to her advantage. Julie is a top-notch recruiter for her firm and was instrumental in saving her company over $250,000 in agency and hiring fees. In September 1996, Julie was featured in an article in *HR Magazine*, which has a circulation of over 40,000 hiring individuals. Julie used the strategy of making copies of this article and sending them to key decision makers at the corporate headquarters. When her company streamlined their human resource department, not only did Julie keep her job, she got a raise to boot! In addition to many of her industry peers seeing the article, so did other writers. As a result, Julie was interviewed by two other magazines.

Television and Radio

After you've experienced some publicity in print, you may decide to explore television and radio. Keep in mind that, as with all media channels, people by the thousands are attempting to get some exposure. Not only is it important to have expertise and credibility in your field, you must also be creative.

Shortly after I decided to approach the television media, I noticed an article about a local individual who had partnered with CNBC to launch a program called *The Career Television Network*. I read this article with great interest and wrote the founder of the company a congratulatory letter. In this letter, I sincerely told him how I admired his courage in pursuing his dream. I also included some background information on myself and explained that I would be eager to help him in any way. Several weeks later, I received a telephone call from him asking to meet me. We hit it off, and I agreed to appear on an upcoming episode as a "career strategist." This program aired at 4:30 A.M., central time, and I knew that not too many people would be watching. However, I determined that it would be a great learning experience and I could use the tape to get other television interviews.

My appearance went well, and I was asked to do another show. One appearance led to another, and I soon became a regular. I learned quite a lot during those tapings, and even though I don't think a single viewer actually saw me (other than friends and family whom I convinced to get up that early—not one of them knew how to program a VCR), I was able to compile a series of interviews, have them edited, and later send that tape along with my press release.

It took over two years and several other local programs before I had accumulated enough experience to land a segment on the *TODAY* show. Once I had the *TODAY* show tape, it was much easier to get other major television programs interested. You can use the same strategy for radio as well.

Worldwide Publicity

Another publicity vehicle is the Internet. Every day, new opportunities are springing up to get your name and expertise in front of millions of people. By using your creativity, perseverance, and skill in self-promotion, you can establish yourself as a credible expert in your field. Not only will you enjoy the rewards of your efforts, but you can help educate others at the same time. *You don't have to be a celebrity in order to benefit from media exposure.* You can set your own limits of what you choose to be a part of. Whatever medium you decide to pursue, however, be sure to be prepared, know your material, take it one step at a time, and by all means have fun with it!

Checklist for Moving On

	Yes	No
1. Have you written down three qualities that you admire about yourself?	___	___
2. Have you practiced acknowledging these qualities?	___	___
3. Have you written a statement to celebrate yourself and begun to share it with others?	___	___
4. Have you practiced accepting and giving compliments each day?	___	___
5. Have you replaced the word *but* with *and* in your vocabulary?	___	___
6. Have you laid a foundation of relationship building in your company, close circle of friends, and business associates?	___	___
7. Have you taken action by volunteering, writing, and so on?	___	___
8. Have you taken a risk and spoken in front of a group or signed up for a public speaking course?	___	___
9. Have you developed a professional press release?	___	___
10. Have you submitted your press release to the proper channels?	___	___
11. Have you begun developing relationships with external contacts?	___	___

▶ 7 ◀

The Educational Edge

Taking Advantage of Lifelong Learning

**Opportunity . . . often it comes disguised
in the form of misfortune, or temporary defeat.**
Napoleon Hill

Have you ever heard a friend or coworker complain about change? It might start out innocently enough with a comment or observation. Then, regardless of how positively you respond, you may notice how determined some people are to focus on projected problems. Soon enough, you realize that your friend has turned into a complete grinch.

"My boss was transferred to another department."

"That's good, isn't it? Does that mean you'll be promoted?"

"No, it means I'll be getting a new boss whom I will have to teach how to do the job."

"Are there parts of your job that you really like to do? Maybe this would be a good time to show the new boss what you excel in. Maybe your old boss didn't notice. Or maybe this would be a good time to get a fresh start redefining your responsibilities to suit your interests more. The new boss will probably be pretty open to suggestions while she's settling in."

"She'll probably want to make us do things the way they did them in her old department. I won't even know how to order supplies anymore."

A good response after a comment like this might simply be, "You'll learn," but often, this is the last thing the other person wants to hear. Most of our adult population complains about work-related stress. Periodic stress can cause fatigue, nervous stomachs, headaches, or even trigger snack attacks and unconscious *evasive behavior tactics*. Chronic stress, however, can lead to hypertension and serious illness.

What's stress about? Science books and popular magazines will tell you that feeling "stress" is triggered by the demands we put on ourselves, psychologically and physically, when we have to adapt to change. Since we're not living in the jungle or in a war zone, we're usually not coming face-to-face with threats to our lives so much as *threats to the way we've been living*.

But change is a way of life, isn't it? We must decide how to deal with change, as we will always be "adapting" to something. We have two choices. What is yours? Suffering from stress, or staying stuck in patterns that don't give you the results you desire. It really boils down to your attitude about **learning.** That's what adapting is, learning how to do something or learning how to do something differently.

Adopting a Learning Attitude

If the friend or coworker from the last example would have been turned off by hearing, "You'll learn," chances are he or she doesn't have a healthy attitude about learning. *Seeing all situations as learning opportunities is a definite boost to your mental health.* Scientists are even recognizing intellectual curiosity (enjoying the pursuit of learning) as a characteristic of people who live long lives.

The ability to learn is not confined to age, formal schooling, your social status, or how much money you make. The process of learning is not much different for adults than it is for children, except that adults usually have a better idea of what they want to learn (based on what they've already experienced), and children usually have to learn what people tell them is important.

How do you feel about learning something new? Are you excited about challenges? Do you like to relate new information to things you already know or do well? Do you usually resist doing something differently? Do you look at doing something differently as a sign that you've been doing something wrong or that you've just been doing it based on what you knew or learned at a different time? Are you afraid to experiment with new things or ideas because they might not work out?

How often have you suffered a setback, personally or professionally, and reviewed the situation to see what you could learn from your experience? Have you ever looked at a sale you didn't make or a speech that didn't go well and decided to try something a little differently to get a better result next time? When you're willing to say, "I don't know, but I can learn" as a response to a challenge, you've overcome one of the biggest blocks keeping many people stuck.

Lifelong Learning Requires Personal Honesty and "Baby Steps"

Admitting when you don't know something, getting truly honest with yourself so that you can determine what exactly you choose to know or do, and then giving yourself a little time to plan how to make progress toward an objective is an important sequence in the lifelong learning process. No matter where you are in life, what your job is about, what your hobbies are, or what obstacles may be part of your current situation, you'll always be coming back to these basic steps.

I have developed countless professional opportunities for myself (where others have gotten stuck) because I don't have any trouble admitting, "Hey, I don't know how to do this." When I was a recruiter, if I recognized that I was missing a piece of information or lacked a certain kind of experience, I refused to pretend otherwise. Instead of acting as if I knew something I didn't so that I wouldn't look stupid, I'd just go about locating resources that would bring me up to speed. Sometimes I've joked that I got my first book published because I didn't know I couldn't—I didn't know that the obstacles were supposed to be practically impossible. I just looked at my goal of getting a book published as an incredible learning opportunity. I kept my goal in mind and methodically went about figuring out what I needed to know or do in order to get there.

The importance of being honest with yourself cannot be underestimated when creating a plan for learning something. Honesty is not just admitting when you don't know something, for it also involves recognizing *what you're willing to do to get it.*

My business is not to remake myself, but make the absolute best of what God made.
Robert Browning

Have you ever expressed an interest in a subject and discovered an expert willing to teach you more than you might care to know? I once told a computer-savvy friend that I desired to learn about the Internet. My goals were pretty much confined to doing research, sending e-mail, and advertising my consulting business. Since my friend's expertise and enthusiasm were as big as the national debt, he assumed I was gearing up for private tutoring that could have kept us both indoors for months. I decided to clarify exactly what I wanted to know and why.

In a way, it was great to have to explain this to someone because it helped me understand my own intentions. Even after I identified my own (less-ambitious-than-my-teacher's) goals, I had to ask myself what I was genuinely willing to do to get this knowledge. How much time was I willing to invest in it? Did I desire to learn how to program and design my own home page, or did I choose to save my time for replying to the thousands of respondents I was expecting to hear from? If you're not honest with yourself about what you are willing to do to get a degree, to learn how to surf the Internet, to learn how to ski, or . . . (I'm sure you can fill in your own goals here), you probably won't succeed in getting there.

Embarking on a learning adventure when you are not fully committed, unfortunately, is a great way to avoid success. Setting a goal without determining a set of specific and manageable actions that can move you closer to your goal is asking for trouble. We talked about the Ten Tiny Steps in Chapter 1. They are especially important when it comes to creating a *learning plan.* Taking baby steps toward mastering new information or skills is crucial if you wish to avoid getting discouraged. Building a history of unsuccessful attempts at learning new things has a terrible way of destroying your confidence about your ability to learn. If you don't operate within a realistic framework, you might start thinking like a grinch, dreading change of any sort and avoiding learning opportunities instead of seeking them out.

When Style Counts

Do you know much about your *personal learning style* and *motivations* for learning? Whether you are seeking an advanced degree or special certification, or taking a course to improve your image or communications skills, understanding your own learning style will help you choose action steps, within a learning plan, that will work for you.

I graduated from high school in three years. I couldn't wait to get out. I thought the class structure stifled creativity and motivation. I knew there were certain "basics" appropriately learned in high school, but there seemed to be too much of an emphasis on names and dates and things that didn't seem very relevant to living my life. At the time, I felt I knew it all. Obviously there couldn't be much to learn from some old textbook that had been etched into the curriculum for the past 20 years. That's what I thought. I didn't know it then, but my expectations of learning were already becoming pretty well formed and pretty "adult." For me, subjects needed to relate to my real-world experience, or I wasn't interested in putting forth much effort.

After I got some work experience, I decided to take a few college courses. I was more motivated to learn because I had more personal experiences to relate to this new information. This experience with formal education was a little better than high school but not an overwhelming success. My first course was taught by a foreign instructor. I remember getting hung up on his accent and looking for signs that this was a rehash of high school, with the exception that I was now paying hard-earned dollars for it. As it turned out, I didn't complete a degree program at the time. (I renewed my commitment to on-the-job learning.) I did succeed, though, in learning a lot about how *I like to learn*, my learning style, which has helped me develop my own personal learning plan. I realized that:

► I like acquiring new information or skills that I can use right away.

► I'm not fond of formal class structures. I have always preferred to learn things as quickly or as slowly as seemed right for me.

These are important discoveries to make about yourself. Now that there are more options for how you might learn something, you can choose methods that suit your learning style. There are countless courses you can take at universities or community colleges, or through company-sponsored professional seminars. You can learn via computer tutorials or even audiotapes that you can play in your car. You can find personal tutors and coaches for developing presentation skills or playing tennis. Even if you need certification or special credentials in a particular field, there may be an option suited to your personal style. All it takes is the willingness to do the necessary research.

Developing a Lifelong Learning Plan— A Balanced Approach

In the very beginning of *Success 2000*, we did some brainstorming on values and beliefs so that we could understand what motivates us, and notice what kinds of things might keep us stuck in patterns that don't allow us to get what we desire. It's important to keep things in perspective, though. Getting what we desire out of life is more than developing a track record for accomplishing goals. The *good stuff* is really about enjoying our accomplishments and appreciating the adventures that take us to them.

Learning can be a pleasure! It can be one of the greatest pleasures in life. (Babies learn new things practically every minute and seem to enjoy life pretty thoroughly.) Although it's easy to get caught up in setting career-oriented learning goals, we can also incorporate plans to learn things for pleasure, personal enrichment, or "just because" reasons, so that life itself does not become drudgery. It's very important to balance the kinds of learning experiences we might pursue.

Nina Mauritz is an interior design consultant with a specialty in food service operations. From the late '80s, when she worked as a designer for a large food service company, through the last six years as an independent, she made it a point to attend single-day seminars on different topics related to her field. One of the key messages of these seminars, she told me, was that "to stay competitive, you had to be able to draw with a computer. If architects or designers were not using the computers now, (according to the seminar sponsors) in three to five years their businesses would suffer." This message was reinforced by her experience in the marketplace. Two to three years ago, she explained, she lost a contract because she wasn't using computer-aided design (CAD).

Very much a self-starter, Nina bought a computer and tried self-study using different books on the subject. While making some progress on her own, she decided to get formal instruction on the skills and then develop a plan to incorporate what she learned into her work. (If you don't put what you learn into practice, she confessed after previous experience with computer classes, it can be quickly forgotten.) She investigated the curriculum at a local junior college, which included both introductory courses on CAD and options for special coursework in different disciplines—CAD for Architects, CAD for Designers, and so on. During the summer, the curriculum calendar was condensed, and she attended a four-hour class twice each week and invested an additional 20 hours per week in homework. This was not a small commitment but certainly one that made a big impact. "Once you learn something, you become more confident. Then, you realize you're ready for the next career step," she said.

After completing her introductory class, she was enthusiastic about enrolling in computer drawing classes for her field. She also found herself motivated to take another course at the junior college. This time it would be just for fun. This course, it turned out, had a big impact on her life, and career, too. The course was called "The Effect You Have on Others," and it used different personality tests to explore personal characteristics and motivations that underlie making positive life changes. The course promoted a "think-feel-do" formula, noting that unless people think *and* feel the same way about an option, they will not be motivated to action. This just-for-fun class, in some ways, taught a life skill. Understanding that people have very different motivations and recognizing the importance of seeing people fully experience their feelings before expecting them to act on something helped Nina in countless situations with clients.

There's a lot to learn from Nina's story:

► Be aware of changes in your industry and make plans to learn new skills or pick up certain credentials *before* they become an absolute requirement for doing business in your field. Know what skills and degrees are required in your field.
► Know your own learning style and understand the challenges involved in mastering each new skill, so that you can make good

decisions regarding how best to learn. Sometimes nothing will replace a classroom experience.

▶ Do your homework when selecting a course, program, or teacher. You may surprise yourself how close you can get to finding exactly what you're looking for.

▶ Be open to taking courses or following up on learning opportunities as they present themselves. Follow hunches. Often, pursuing "just because" learning opportunities can help you develop life skills that you may not have expected.

▶ Reward yourself for your efforts. Balance your pursuit of career-oriented learning with learning that encourages self-discovery and pleasure.

It's funny, sometimes, to think about how important report cards seemed to be when we were children. Even as adults, if we take college-credit courses or find ourselves pursuing advanced degrees, it's hard not to think about how our performance might be measured. Of course, as adults we have a great opportunity to develop our own "learning cards," which, instead of someone else's *reporting*, can be geared to *reflecting* our own passions and interests. A "learning card" can guide us in making plans and taking action.

Let's take a minute to design a Lifelong Learning Card that will keep us on a path of learning for survival and growth. Then we can look at specific resources and considerations that may be part of using this tool. (Use a lined index card or a piece of notebook paper. I also suggest using a pencil; you may be making revisions regularly, perhaps every year.)

1. The first question you might ask yourself is what do you **choose** to know or be able to do. It might be advisable to keep your list down to six to ten things. (If you don't know what you desire to learn, but you do know you choose to improve your position in the job market, refer to Chapter 12 for places to go to get ideas.)

2. After you've jotted down several learning objectives, you must look at each of them and evaluate whether that objective would satisfy career development, personal interests, or health and self-discovery themes. If there is not some balance in the numbers of goals in each area, you might want to rethink some of your learning objectives. You can always put them back into your plan later.

3. Review each goal again. What might be required of you to get there? Here's where you may choose to do research and think about your personal learning style. Sometimes a goal may involve several steps or options. Sometimes a goal may require only one step.

4. Write down at least one action step for each goal—something you are ready to do now to reach that goal. (You may even decide to give yourself a time frame for your action steps.) If you're not ready to commit to doing anything at all, this might be a good time to re-examine the goal and perhaps shelve it for another time.

You certainly don't want to feel overwhelmed by your learning card, but sometimes the act of writing things down very simply firms up our thoughts and intentions. A Lifelong Learning Card might look something like this:

What I choose to learn	Why learning this is important (for career, personal interests, self-discovery/growth)	What might be required (options)	What action steps I will take (time frame)
1.		a. b. c.	1. 2.
2.		a. b. c.	1. 2.
3.		a. b. c.	1. 2.
4.		a. b. c.	1. 2.
5.		a. b. c.	1. 2.
6.		a. b. c.	1. 2.

Perhaps you decide to pursue an MBA. Let's say you have an undergraduate degree in a technical field and enjoy your industry, but you don't have the business background necessary for management positions. Or maybe you're considering changing jobs, moving from a family-operated business to a more structured corporation with better benefits, and you desire the type of educational credentials that would complement your practical experience. This is obviously a career-oriented goal. What might you have to do to get there?

Now you must do some research. What kinds of educational programs are available to you locally? Can you attend night or weekend classes? If you can't alter your work schedule much to accommodate classwork, will your family be able to help you with other obligations? Have you completed any course work that could be applied to this degree? How will you pay for school? Does your company have a tuition reimbursement policy? Does this policy carry any restrictions? Asking yourself these kinds of questions will clue you in to the steps involved in reaching this goal and suggest specific action steps you could take immediately (i.e., sending away for course catalogs, checking out potential travel conflicts in your current position, etc.).

What if one of your goals is learning how to ski? A "getting there" strategy might be to find an instructor and schedule time to do it. Your action steps might include checking out ski clubs or travel packages that provide instruction, getting information from friends on how they learned, or buying gear (sometimes making a financial investment can turn *talk about goals* into actual pursuit).

Use the Lifelong Learning Card to think about some of your goals. Practice thinking through all four steps. Make sure your goals represent a balance between career, currently identified interests, and more open-ended personal growth (where you might not actually be sure *what* you will learn).

Learning for Earning

What if you are not sure what you desire to learn, especially when it comes to your career? How are you supposed to know what you should know? You may have to ask yourself: "What kinds of education or skills do people in my field have? If I decide to make a career change, what credentials will it require? What skills do I need to be the best in my field and convince an employer to hire me?"

The job market, we're reminded constantly, is extremely competitive. As we discussed in Chapter 5, technology is becoming an important part of more and more jobs. In fact, learning how to use technology within a particular field might be looked at as a pretty basic learning requirement. And operating in a global environment means that people are increasingly interdependent. It's becoming more and more important to have a better understanding of what other people do and to learn skills that will help us interface with others. Learning these so-called soft skills used to be passed over as secondary to gaining technical expertise; however, they are becoming vital to ensure that departments, companies, business partnerships, and other systems operate at their best.

There are a lot of ways you can **research** what types of things you could focus your learning efforts on in a given field. Here is my Top Ten list (with apologies to David Letterman) of places you might go to identify career-oriented learning goals.

1. Have you made it a point to attend career seminars or job fairs? Talking candidly to recruiters who specialize in your field can provide you with valuable insight into what employers are looking for, and they may be able to advise you on how you might get up to speed as quickly as possible. Keep an eye on your local paper. When you do attend an event, keep your perspective and take the pressure off. You're there to learn what you have to do to get the job you desire, not necessarily walk home with an offer.

2. Do you take advantage of educational opportunities that are sponsored by your company (outside of specific job training)? Remember Nina's story? Sometimes a short-term experience can bring desirable long-term options into the forefront. Single-day seminars may point out other courses to pursue. Are internships or externships available to you for exploring your career options?

3. Do you belong to any professional associations? Do you know the major associations in your field? One of the primary functions of professional associations is to promote professional standards and support educational programs for their members. If you don't belong to your field's association, you can still use the *Encyclopedia of Associations* (Detroit: Gale Research, 1996), available at your library, to look up associations that may support your profession. Generally, they will answer questions on educational requirements and standards in the field.

4. Do you talk to people in your field? Notice what education or certification they have. Ask your boss what it might take for you to get ahead. (This will also show your drive.)

5. Have you met with a qualified career counselor? Advisers from any schools you've attended, or professionals listed in the yellow pages, should be able to advise you on educational requirements within the field you wish to enter.

6. Have you checked *The Occupational Outlook Handbook* (Washington, D.C.: U.S. Department of Labor, 1996). Put out by the Bureau of Labor Statistics, it is a wealth of information. It's helpful for looking at your own field, and it's a great resource for when you might be contemplating a career change. Each occupation category includes not only a description of basic tasks and functions associated with the job but also a section called "Training and Other Qualifications for Advancement." Maybe you will choose to move into teaching or to become an airline pilot. This book will provide information on immediate licensing requirements and often notes professional standards on continuing education.

7. Have you read the want ads? Okay, it can be a drag to look through the want ads when you're seriously hunting. However, it can be a great adventure if you're all right with where you are but would like to figure out where you desire to go next. Want ads will usually include degree or certification requirements along with desired experience. Just as important, job descriptions will usually highlight "competencies" a person in the job would be expected to demonstrate. As we move more toward competency-based education (more on this later), knowing what skills and areas of expertise are valued in a given position will guide the development of your learning objectives (and even help you write your resume).

8. Do you receive course catalogs? Do you look forward to getting mail-order gift catalogs? They're usually fun to read because they're full of ideas and there's no pressure to buy anything. If you're going to develop a lifelong learning plan, you might like to get on a few select mailing lists for course catalogs. Universities, community colleges, national seminar companies (Dun & Bradstreet, National Seminars, Fred Pryor, etc.) and large national associations will usually send you a course catalog at no charge. More often than not, each course description will include information on who should take the course and how they will benefit, list primary learning objectives, and note how the course might be part of a larger program for a degree or for professional certification.

9. Have you visited your favorite book palace? Whether in a local library or a bookstore, space devoted to career books is on the rise.

10. Have you surfed the Internet? Hype or hope, there's a lot of debate about the value of going on-line. When it comes to career and educational assistance, however, its potential is enormous. Most on-line services include special areas for job and career interests. There are over 10,000 job sites on the World Wide Web. Jobtrak (http://www.jobtrak.com) is in the top 5% of most frequently visited sites. While many of the job-related sites are devoted to job hunting, several Web sites can also be used to point out valuable educational goals in different fields. Various on-line magazines offer features related to preparation for different fields, and on-line forums allow you to post questions regarding careers and receive input and advice from people all over the world.

If these 10 questions don't help you formulate a short-term game plan for learning, consider taking seminars or longer programs covering a soft skill. There are certain skills hiring authorities evaluate positively regardless of what position you might be interested in within their company. We talked about the '90s as being a decade of fast-paced change and a global business environment. Skills that are readily applicable to different kinds of jobs—transferable skills—expand your opportunities not only within the job market at large but also within a department or company, so they increase your value to your current employer as well. The following list of "competencies" (posted by Career Services of Bowling Green State University [http://www.bgsu.edu/offices/careers/process/competen.html]) represents demonstrable skills that can be considered great foundations for both career and life learning:

▶ Planning and organizational skills.
▶ Oral and written communications skills.
▶ Decision-making, supervisory, management and/or leadership skills.
▶ Financial management skills.
▶ Critical thinking, problem solving, and conflict-resolution skills.
▶ Teamwork and team-building skills.
▶ Ethics and tolerance skills.
▶ Personal and professional management skills.
▶ Transferable skills:
  —Information management.
  —Design and planning skills.
  —Research and investigation skills.
  —Communications skills.
  —Human relations and interpersonal skills.
  —Management and administrative skills.
  —Valuing skills.
  —Personal and career development skills.

A Different Kind of School

To learn is to live; to cease to learn is to die.
Anonymous

Once you identify some of the things you choose to learn or skills you choose to master, you can begin to figure out where you can get this education and how you can arrange your schooling to fit into your lifestyle.

Many corporations offer a certain amount of elective training such as presentation skills classes or leadership programs as company benefits. These kinds of courses can usually be taken on company time or scheduled to avoid conflicts with other job or family obligations.

Community colleges are growing, too, and changing their image from a place to go if you can't get into a four-year school to an institution that supports continuing education for career-oriented people. In general, curriculums at community colleges reflect adult learning principles. Remember how I had problems with "names and dates" classes because they just didn't seem relevant to what I needed to know to do my job better? Although many traditional four-year university programs continue to focus on theory and concepts, more and more curriculums are being designed to develop competencies that have immediate applications in the workforce. Students like this orientation because they have the opportunity to put into practice what they've learned and to see results right away. Employers appreciate this orientation because it places the emphasis on preparing people to do what employers require in a particular job. The learning curve for new employees is dramatically reduced.

DeVry, Inc., which offers bachelor's degrees in a variety of technical and business-oriented fields, and its affiliate Keller Management School, which offers advanced degrees in specific management disciplines, might best represent a new trend in education. DeVry, Inc., is a publicly traded company that treats its educational programs like *products* that need to provide *value* for its customers, the people who pay tuition. Value, in this case, is measured by impact in the workforce. There are 17 DeVry campuses in the United States and Canada and 19 Keller locations (all of which offer the same curriculum).

Pat Kapper, dean of academic affairs for DeVry, confirms that their approach is different from that of many four-year universities: From the beginning of any bachelor's program, "We promote education as a lifelong process. A bachelor's degree is just a first step. It's a foregone conclusion, especially in technology fields, that each student will be continuing their education after getting their degree."

Both DeVry and Keller offer the following advantages:

► They are oriented to the desires of adult learners. Most Keller students are employed full-time. Scheduling is flexible, and by intent Keller tries to recognize the value of the real-world experiences each student brings to class.

► They provide applications-oriented educations. By creating "lab" settings and supporting co-op programs (scheduled arrangements for working part-time while attending school), DeVry stays focused on preparing students for the job market. Keller's current management degree programs (master of business administration, master in project management, and master in human resource development) and their curriculums reflect very close dialogue with the business community. These schools recognize the importance of providing students with skills that employer-sponsors can see put to use immediately, especially since most students (80%) receive some form of tuition reimbursement.

▶ They utilize "practitioners" as faculty. All faculty must have on-the-job experience in the field they are teaching. This excites students because it gives them the opportunity to learn from those who, in addition to being able to answer textbook questions, are also people doing what the students aspire to do. Tim Ricordati, dean of Keller Management School, calls this the Twinkle Factor. Keller requires instructors to have 10 years of business experience with a proven record of success in their functional area. More importantly, they must also be motivated to share what they know. Instructors are selected based on how enthusiastic and passionate they are about their subject. "When you can see the sparkle in their eyes, and notice how they want to talk about their subject all the time—as if it was the most important and interesting thing in the world—that's when the subject matter comes alive."

Do you remember some of your least-favorite teachers? They might have been hard graders or maybe they just stood in front of your classroom like a talking head spouting off. Have you ever had teachers who inspired you because they loved their subject and loved learning?

Demonstrating What You Know

If you've started working on your lifelong learning plan with an emphasis on career goals, you'll also need to decide how to demonstrate what you know to your employer, to potential employers, or to clients (if you work independently). If you decide to show clients your personal commitment to continual improvement, don't be bashful about sending the local papers press releases that mention special degrees or certifications you've earned. Include them in your marketing materials. (See Chapter 6.)

Glenn Gienko, Motorola executive vice president and director of human resources, has shared several insights on trends in recruiting and offered some tips on how to demonstrate knowledge or competency in a particular area to a particular employer. Motorola is a large, diversified employer that has a strong record promoting ongoing education and personal development. One of the things the company evaluates in candidates for all types of positions is their ability to adapt to change. Glenn Gienko states, "Our recruitment process, regardless of position, is usually a 10- to 12-step process. It includes personality and aptitude tests. We're looking for people who can read, write and reason, notice details and show dedication. We assess a candidate's ability to deal with change. If they are *change resistant*, even if they have some good credentials, there's a good chance they will get sick or be unhappy working here. That wouldn't do either of us any good."

Although the majority of Motorola's recruitment activities (especially for engineering and marketing) is oriented to college recruitment, it has done considerable research and developed systems that help to predict the success of new hires in the roles they are recruited for. Using what may become another trend for larger corporations, Motorola utilizes elaborate resume scanning software to sort databases of job applicants. The software notices key words and can perform searches for candidates based on multiple criteria.

Based on Glenn's experience with this tool, he offers a few suggestions for demonstrating formal education and life-experience learning:

▶ A college degree is fairly important. Although the possibility of hiring nondegreed applicants is not eliminated, a college degree is often the basis for first-round sorting.

▶ Get familiar with the competencies required for a particular job and use industry terminology in your resume.

▶ Don't underestimate the importance of soft skills. Even for technical jobs, employers want to see terms like *team player, excellent oral and written communication skills*, and so on.

▶ Go beyond the "results-achievements" formula. If you are going to include statistics or quantify accomplishment, briefly explain **how** you achieved your results (i.e., through managing other people, by designing a new process, etc.)

▶ Use your resume to give as complete and honest a description of yourself as possible. Include continuing education initiatives, hobbies, and things you've learned by being a volunteer or active community member.

The Other Stuff

We've spent a lot of time talking about how to research learning ob-jectives and action steps involved in career-oriented learning. Get-ting ideas so that you can make plans to pursue hobbies or take advantage of opportunities for self-discovery probably will come much easier. What might be important to mention, though, is that giving yourself the time to include other types of learning pursuits in your life might take some thought. You might consider actually tak-ing a sabbatical or break from your job, so that you can explore your special interests. Sometimes, taking time off can reenergize a career.

If you have fantasies of taking six months off to backpack in Kazakhstan, start a home-based business, or train horses, pick up Hope Dlugozima's *Six Months Off—How to Plan, Negotiate, and Take the Break You Deserve without Burning Bridges or Going Broke* (New York: Henry Holt, 1996). It covers everything from getting in touch with your sabbatical fantasies to researching optimal times and costs for planning your getaway to the best way to present a proposal to an employer.

Checklist for Moving On

	Yes	No
1. When you consider a learning goal, are you honest with yourself about what you would be willing to do to accomplish that goal?	——	——
2. Do you understand your own learning style? Do you prefer tackling something new independently or do you prefer learning as part of a group process?	——	——
3. Are you able to identify a balanced number of learning goals related to career pursuits, known personal interests, and self-discovery?	——	——
4. Do you do any of the following regularly: look at the want ads just to see what's out there, receive course catalogs from different schools or training companies, look at career books at libraries or bookstores, or take advantage of elective seminars offered by current employers?	——	——

Checklist (*continued*)

	Yes	No
5. Have you spent much time or devoted much attention to developing soft skills? Are you including types of creative expression within your learning plan?	___	___
6. Have you taken action to learn something new?	___	___
7. Do you embrace the idea that every time you learn something, you will be adding to or changing your learning plan?	___	___

► 8 ◄

Taking the "Work" Out of Networking

A stranger is a friend I have not met yet.
Anonymous

My first experience with "structured" networking was a nightmare! I had always felt most effective in a one-to-one scenario and was terrified of group situations. In order to build the staff and client base of the new agency I was in charge of, I forced myself to join our local chamber of commerce. The owner of our company suggested that I attend the chamber's weekly networking meeting.

In the room where the event was being held, I stuck close to the door and practically pressed myself up against the wall, hoping not to be noticed! I was petrified. Not only did I not approach anyone, my glaring frown scared everyone away—except Charlie, the insurance agent. Like a Tasmanian devil whirling at top speed, Charlie pumped my hand and slipped me his business card all in one short second. He then started talking a mile a minute (though he never did inquire about my career), barely taking enough time to catch his breath. Within three minutes he completed his barrage of comments and excused himself to prey on another helpless newcomer.

In that moment, I decided I hated networking. Not only could I never do what Charlie had just done, I would never use his insurance agency either. I left that night feeling like a failure. I had three business cards of potential leads but a pocket full of my own cards that I never got around to passing out.

The next morning when I arrived at work, I took out the three business cards I had picked up, the attendance list from the event, and the chamber of commerce directory. I decided to write a letter to everyone who had attended the event. I was convinced that these people would be happy to get my correspondence and "network" with me. Boy, was I ever wrong! Not only did I fail to get a single response, I was hung up on more times than if I had been making cold calls.

I was stumped! If networking wasn't the answer, how could I possibly develop my business? I decided that although I could benefit from networking, I would do it differently. I asked myself several questions that laid the groundwork for how I could be myself and still be successful in gathering leads and generating new business. I found my answer in the Golden Rule: "Do unto others as you would have them do unto you."

What is a network anyway? What is networking? A *network is a group of interconnected relationships*. Wouldn't you agree that relationships are one of the most important things in your life? Think about the relationships you currently have. Of course, you are born with family relationships, but throughout your life you have pushed beyond your family circle to build new relationships. We don't often think about how we made friends when we were kids because it seemed to happen naturally. However, developing relationships comes down to pretty much the same thing at any age: finding people you feel you can connect with. Building a personal and professional network is just like making friends when you were a child. Only now you can do it with a sense of purpose and have fun as well.

Networking is purposefully creating interconnected relationships that enhance your life and the lives of others. Decide to view networking as a process instead of an event. Stay unattached to the immediate outcome and expect that only good will come out of your connections. By taking off the pressure of being attached to the outcome (or attempting to meet a certain quota), you'll truly enjoy relationship building and you'll take the limits off what "should" happen. Placing less pressure on yourself and others creates sincere, fun, and often lifelong relationships, which in turn bring success. A process is not a single act or one dialogue. It's not something you do **to** someone. It's something you do **with** someone.

Creating Relationships to Enhance Your Career and Personal Success

Establishing good relationships is at the center of every productive networking encounter. The following list contains some of the key elements of a good relationship:

1. Discovering what you have in common with the other person.
2. A feeling of trust and genuineness.
3. An interest in learning more about each other.
4. Feeling comfortable with each other and being able to converse easily.
5. Being motivated to create a win-win situation (and being willing to put the time into building and maintaining a relationship).

Why is it that some people seem to make new friendships easily while others struggle so? When I first started to network, I felt extremely uneasy being in a group setting. I was so focused on how I was *different* from everyone else that I didn't take the time to discover what I had in common with them. My thoughts and beliefs created my reality. What is your reality?

Write down three current beliefs you have about networking and then write down three new beliefs that may give you more positive results. Example: "I am shy and everyone else here is so outgoing." Replace this belief with "Although I am often quiet, this helps me to be a good listener. Today I will look for ways to focus on how I am *like* others rather than how I am *different*. I will celebrate my good listening skills and look for ways to engage others by asking questions."

The only way to discover commonalities with others is to learn to ask questions. Many of us have made the mistake of talking too much to cover up our nervousness or insecurities. **We can't learn anything while we are talking.** Study the following tips and action steps to creating good relationships with others:

Seven Key Elements to Creating Good Relationships with Others

1. Not doing all the talking.
2. Asking thought-provoking and open-ended positive questions such as:
   —What excites you most about your career?

—Who inspired you to do what you are doing?

—You are so passionate about _____ . Tell me more.

3. Listening with interest and 100% of your attention.
4. Giving feedback on what you've heard and learned.
5. Volunteering information about yourself, focusing on what you have in common.
6. Making notes, after meeting, about what you've learned (birthdays, anniversaries, spouses' names, children, anything of interest to your contacts). Keep these notes in your database, card file, or calendar to use as a reference during your follow-up.
7. Taking the time to follow up with new contacts. (It's better to meet 10 new people and follow up with all 10 than to meet 100 people and follow up with 1.)

Now write down at least five questions you can ask people to learn more about them and to engage them in conversation. Next, reflect on a few situations in which you met new people and the exchange wasn't all that positive or productive. Did you follow the above steps? Congratulate yourself for those steps you did follow. Which ones did you leave out? Now don't beat up on yourself—instead, plan what you can do differently next time. Mistakes are only bad if you don't learn from them!

In his book *How to Win Friends and Influence People* (revised edition; New York: Pocket Books, 1982), one of the best-selling books of all time, Dale Carnegie tells the story of a dinner party he attended where he met a botanist. Dale had never talked with a botanist before and found him fascinating. The botanist spoke for almost four hours straight while Dale listened intently. At the end of the evening the botanist turned to the party's host and exclaimed that Mr. Carnegie was such an interesting and stimulating conversationalist! Dale, who heard this exchange, was surprised as he had barely spoken two words all evening.

How many times have you found yourself in a similar situation? We all desire this kind of attention from others. However, you must first learn to give it. (If you haven't already enjoyed reading *How to Win Friends and Influence People*, I suggest getting a copy—it's a must for anyone looking to create wonderful new relationships.) This discussion leads us to the next step in building relationships—learning to promote others first.

The Art of "Promoting Others First"

We live in such a "me first" society that it's truly an art when people learn how to develop relationships by initially giving before receiving. Let me give you a good example of how promoting others first will benefit you greatly.

I received in the mail one day an unsolicited newsletter that caught my attention. After reading a very interesting story about how to get free publicity, I proceeded to write a letter to Ms. Kent, the author of the article, telling her how much I enjoyed her writing style and what I had learned. I also enclosed my business card and some information about myself. About a week later, I received a call from her. She informed me that she was in charge of a writers' group that needed a speaker for the following week. Would I be interested? Having a previous commitment, I politely declined; however, I offered to make a couple of calls to see whom I could engage for her.

Within 15 minutes I had gathered the names of three people who were possibilities, and I placed phone calls to them. I telephoned Ms. Kent to give names, phone numbers, and a brief background on each of these three people. She was quite surprised and pleased with what I had done. By the end of the conversation, she asked me to send her a press kit on myself and a copy of *Getting Hired in the '90s*.

The following week I received a call from Ms. Kent telling me how well the event had gone and that the speaker (one of my three referrals) was terrific. (By the way, the three speakers that I suggested were also quite pleased with me.) Ms. Kent then asked to interview me for an upcoming article for the newspaper column that she was writing. I readily agreed. The newspaper article ran a couple of weeks later, and I received a tremendous amount of business as a result.

Happy with the success that I had had, I decided to write a letter to the editor of the newsletter and explain how Ms. Kent's article impacted my life. Not only was she happy to get this feedback, but she also decided to write an article about my book and business. This article alone brought me several new clients and helped create a good relationship with the editor. In fact, the editor went on to refer me a corporate client for a long-term consulting contract worth over $40,000! (See Figure 8.1.)

The end result of promoting others first is not always new business or additional revenue immediately, so I never *expected* any of this

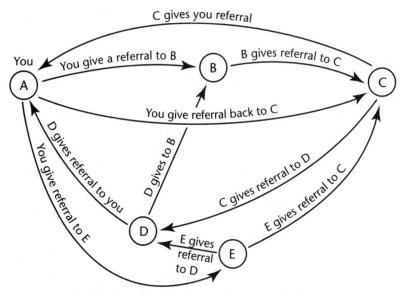

You give three referrals and get back three from all different sources.

Figure 8.1   The Flow of Effective Networking.

to happen. I was just happy to be of some assistance to these people and in return gained some valuable business friendships that I will always treasure. And in addition to receiving new business and publicity from these contacts, I was able to utilize the editing services of Ms. Kent for the second edition of my book.

When learning how to promote others first, you must exercise creativity. Being thoughtful about how someone else might utilize your personal network is a great first step. It shows your willingness to share (a great quality for building a relationship), and demonstrating your understanding of what kinds of connections could help someone else reflects your sensitivity to another's situation. Promoting someone through your personal network doesn't cost anything, and the effort will always come back to you. (Note: It may not always come back directly from the person you assisted. The universe works by cause and effect.)

Often I hear people who are just starting a career, or are switching jobs or industries, mention that they don't have any contacts. This is rarely true! Unless you've been a monk for 10 years and have had no contact with the outside world, you have more contacts than you think. Take the example of Phil Jimenez.

Phil was a recent college graduate who had a degree in political science. I first met him after he approached me at a book signing for *Getting Hired in the '90s*. Phil waited until the group dispersed and then seized the opportunity to network. He politely introduced himself, told me how much he had learned from my talk, and wondered if I had a few minutes to talk with him. I said yes, and we spent the next 15 minutes discussing his career. After learning more about him, I suggested that he call me later that week to see what leads I could give him.

Shortly thereafter, I received a nice card from Phil thanking me for the time I'd spent with him and telling me he would call me later that week. I was impressed with his excellent follow-up and professional etiquette. When he contacted me a couple of days later, I approached Phil about a project I was currently working on. I was willing to offer my career consulting services in exchange for his keeping a daily diary of all his activities. I would use this information for an article I was working on and for my research. He agreed, and we proceeded to engage in several career counseling sessions. Phil was a bright, eager young man willing to try anything new in order to get a great career.

When it came to networking, though, Phil was having difficulty. He didn't believe that he had much to offer others and, therefore, was challenged by "promoting others first." I suggested that Phil list every person and organization that he had ever had any contact with, past or present. Within a couple of hours we had over 50 individuals on his list. I encouraged him to reestablish correspondence with several of his contacts. I explained that he wasn't to come straight out and ask for a job but rather to learn what these people's interests, goals, and needs were currently.

Several days later, Phil called me excitedly and shared a lead with me. HACE (the Hispanic Alliance of Career Enhancement), an organization for which he had volunteered during college, was looking for a speaker, and he wanted to recommend me. I thanked him for the opportunity and assured him that he was indeed on the right track. The referral he gave me worked out very well (I eventually spoke at one of their conferences, sold many books, wrote articles for their newsletter, and met many influential and wonderful people), but more than that, this situation helped build Phil's confidence because he learned that he was able to help people out.

Soon after, Phil landed a great position as a customer satisfaction representative for a Fortune 500 firm. We still stay in contact to this day; in fact, I invited him to speak at one of my events and share with others his story of success. Learn from Phil. Even if you are a recent graduate or new to the networking scene, you know at least one person to begin this process with. Stay positive and focused, and you'll soon see great results.

Some of my best present networking contacts started out with less than remarkable results! One day I received a call in response to an advertisement I had placed in a trade journal (the only response I ever got from that periodical). Tom was in the premium incentive industry and was located on the east coast. After discussing his interest in my book, we decided that it just wasn't a good fit for his needs. However, we had several things in common and started corresponding via fax, e-mail, telephone, and letters. One year later, we still hadn't conducted any business together. But we both hung in there, and when his business started to go in a different direction, so did mine. Finally, we were at a point where we could help one another out. Since that time we have partnered on a major project, and I've used his company for several printing jobs. Although we've never met face-to-face, I count Tom as one of my strongest networking contacts.

I hope you can see by the above success stories how enjoyable and profitable promoting others first can be. It changes the feeling of "using" someone in networking to a feeling of offering something and feeling good about yourself and the situation.

TIPS TO LEARNING THE ART OF "PROMOTING OTHERS FIRST"

► Make a list of contacts and leads (relationships that you've already built). Be sure you reacquaint yourself with these people if you haven't spoken to them in awhile. Needs and goals change all the time; be sure you are up-to-date on what your contacts are working on and looking for.

► Scan business periodicals, newspapers, the Internet, and so on, to gain access to information that your contacts may need. (Clip articles for your contacts or e-mail information that may be of use to them.)

▶ When you are referred to others, *ask what they could use help on before asking for help.* Check your database to see how your connections can help.

▶ Set aside at least one hour per week to stay in contact and update your networking files. (I use ACT software on my PC to do this task; it even has an alarm to notify me when it's time to do follow-up calls.)

▶ Don't give up too easily! It takes time to build relationships, and you may not have something to give right away to everyone you meet.

▶ Finally, make sure to ask for referrals and leads—be specific in telling people what you are doing and what your desires are.

Once you've become good at promoting others, *you must also learn to ask for what you need.* Creating win-win situations is imperative in order to succeed, feel good about what you're doing, make a living, and help others feel good about giving to you as well.

Ask for What You Desire

Recently I realized how lax I'd become in asking for help on expanding my business. (I'm a natural promoter of others—learned perhaps from my recruiting days—and I often forget to ask for help, believing that others will automatically promote me.) A good friend of mine stopped by for coffee, and we started talking business. I gave her several referrals, and she was pleased. At the end of the conversation, I explained what I was doing in my corporate workshops and asked her if she knew anyone who might be interested in hearing more about what I was doing. She immediately perked up and said that her company might be interested and asked if she could take some of my information to her boss. The next day she called me. She had an appointment all set up for me for the following week. Talk about quick action! Barb is one of my best networking sources, and I consider her to be part of my "extended sales force," which leads us to the next stage of taking the "work" out of networking—how to build your own sales force by connecting people. But first, consider the following suggestions that will help you to be successful in receiving solid leads:

Three Criteria for Getting What You Deserve

1. Develop a 30-second "commercial" that sells you and your product or service. Make sure it directly explains what you offer (practice

this statement until you have it memorized). Tell everyone you meet about your business and be enthusiastic—the more excited you are about what you have to offer, the more excited people will be to hear your message.

2. Be specific when asking for referrals. State the type of referral you desire and learn to ask, "**Whom do you know?**" rather than, "Do you know anyone?"

3. Ask for referrals regularly. You are not the top priority for others. They have their own business to consider and will often forget about your desires. Remind them periodically about what you are working on and what is the best referral for you.

Building a "Sales Team" That Works for You

When I changed careers, from recruiting into publishing, I had not a single contact in the publishing industry. Rather than spend years trying to build my contacts (namely because I didn't have the time or cash flow to wait that long), I developed a plan to work smarter not harder. I realized how fun and easy networking could be from my experience with Ms. Kent. I decided to more proactively network (rather than leave it to happenstance) and proceeded to list several key individuals in my industry and influential people in other industries as well.

After I had developed my basic list (10 names of people I had met, read about, or heard about), I called each and every person. With the individuals I had not previously spoken to, I utilized the seven steps to creating a good relationship. As for the people I already had a relationship with, I informed them of my goal to network regularly with a group of professionals who were interested and would take action to promote others in the business community. This wasn't going to be a structured group that would meet weekly, pay dues, or give leads. Instead, I viewed our relationship as an extension to one another's company or business, and due to our tremendously busy schedules, we would conduct our exchanges via fax and e-mail.

Each of these individuals was pleased with this idea because none of us wanted to add another networking event or meeting to our already overcommitted calendars. We agreed to begin slowly and let the process evolve with as little structure as possible. We all viewed this opportunity as employing "sales representatives," without paying commissions. Every group requires some leadership, and I volunteered to begin the process. I typed up a simple form that included the name, addresses (including e-mail), and phone number of each participant. I asked each person to submit a paragraph describing his or her product and services and what made them different.

Once I received this information from the group, I compiled a two-page report with the results and faxed it back to them along with a one-page questionnaire. On this questionnaire, I asked only two questions: (1) What are you currently working on? and (2) What leads or information are you currently looking for? When I received the completed questionnaires, I faxed all this additional information to the 10 members of my "sales force." What happened next was astounding.

A few days later I received calls from several individuals with information—names and opportunities to pursue. Two members of this group explained that they had recently attended appointments with key decision makers, and these meetings had resulted in interest in my company's services. Using the art of promoting others, these individuals were able to get me two interested contacts to pursue.

One of the greatest benefits of this type of networking (third-party endorsement) is the credibility factor you receive before any contact with your potential client. You are able to begin the relationship assured you'll be well received. If your "sales force" has done its job, you can enter the conversation knowing that this client is interested, and you can focus primarily on building the relationship rather than on the time-consuming process of trying to discover if you have a "fit."

The first lead I received from my "sales force" was a recruiter from a Fortune 100 firm. Janet, my "sales rep," had done such a terrific job introducing me at her appointment that by the time I telephoned my lead, he was very excited to hear from me. We agreed to meet for a business breakfast later that week, and afterwards he agreed to go back to the office and convince his boss to use my consulting services. By late afternoon, not only did I have an appointment to meet the general manager (and final decision maker), but he was already presold on me and my services!

I recommend use of this kind of third-party endorsement only if you are convinced that your contact has credibility with the decision maker, understands and can sell your business effectively, and is enthusiastic about doing so. Otherwise, I would recommend going directly to the decision maker.

To make a great story even better, this account hired me to lead a "minisession" (they said this was for budget reasons; however, we both knew it was to check me out first!) for their recruiting force. The session was such a success that the general manager referred me to the corporate headquarters (and presold me quite enthusiastically, I might add), and corporate hired me for an extensive and lucrative consulting assignment. This project gave me the confidence and credibility to pursue other similar assignments and grow my business in a whole new direction!

Building your networking contacts will not only allow you to "survive" the remainder of the '90s and into the turn of the century but also help you to "thrive." Whether you are a business owner or an employee, you can choose to establish long-term influential business relationships and build these contacts into a "sales force" to help you work smarter not harder. By utilizing the relationship-building skills that we have covered thus far, we can now create a plan that will assist you in deriving effective and rewarding results.

All of us have 24 hours in a day. No more, no less. Does the person who earns $250,000 per year work 10 times harder than one who earns $25,000? Probably not. In fact, you'll find many successful businesspeople earning a lucrative salary and taking four vacations per year or spending a great deal of time entertaining on the golf course. So how can you work less and earn more? The answer is by creating an extended circle of influential people around you who are also interested in working smarter not harder. To do just that, follow these steps:

1. Select five individuals (start small and build on this list) whom you already have a connection or rapport with. Contact them and learn about their company, job, interests, and current business problems. If, after learning about them, you decide that they fit your requirements (and you can help them as well), explain that you are looking to increase your business while decreasing the time you "work" at it. Ask them if they would also be interested in benefiting from this. If they are not interested, don't be put off—not everyone is going to see the big picture. Instead ask them, "Who do you know

who is a successful business professional like yourself and may be interested in this kind of referral?" Be sure to get at least one or two leads and be sure to ask if you can mention who referred you when you call these leads.

2. When you have a team of five individuals, decide on how you would like to see this program work. Will it be structured? Nonstructured? Will you speak in person, over the phone, or via e-mail? How often will you stay in contact with one another? Make sure the group will work as a team and that you are not stuck handling all the details—after all, everyone will benefit from this program.

3. Have the team make an agreement to learn about one another's businesses and to go through their existing clients to see if there are any good connections for other members of the team. You will also want to make sure that everyone is willing and able to make appropriate referrals to new potential clients. This program will only work when each party participates fully and is excited and accountable for his or her actions.

4. Spend time working on your plan. Don't look for instant results; instead, view this as a savings account into which you put your money (in this case, your time) and add to it consistently until you finally see the payoff.

5. Periodically review the members of your team. Add new members as time permits and dissolve agreements with those individuals who don't hold up their end of the bargain. Don't be afraid to approach members of your team who are taking more than they are giving. Explain that results are required from them in order to continue with this agreement. If they are not willing or able to participate, let them know that it isn't in anyone's best interest for them to continue at this time. Perhaps, down the road they may want to rejoin the team.

Note: If you work in a company employing many other people, you can also use this procedure internally.

Typically this system works well for entrepreneurs and very self-motivated individuals who do not require a tremendous amount of structure or follow-up. If, however, you would like to create some of the same results but prefer a more structured routine, you can choose a leads group in your local community. Take Michelle Rathman, for example. Michelle is the president of Impact! Communications, Inc., a public relations, marketing, and advertising firm outside of Chicago. Michelle is a member of two local Execunet chapters and serves as president of one.

After fours years of trying to make it in the chamber of commerce networking arena and feeling dismayed and frustrated, Michelle was invited to attend a lunch meeting for one of the Execunet groups. From that point on, she says, her business took a turn for the better. After only three months, 90% of her business came via referrals from fellow members. She has been with the organization for nearly four years now and attributes her dynamic growth to structured networking. "For the first time in my career, I had the opportunity to follow up on a referral without that nervous feeling. The referral had already been told wonderful things about my company, and it wasn't a matter of will you use my firm, but rather, when would you like to get started!"

Michelle adds, "We meet every week to exchange qualified business referrals. I am surrounded by decision makers, people who understand my business, who believe in me and who are enthusiastic about promoting me and my work." The idea behind this type of networking is that you make the meetings an integral part of your work-week—a standing appointment.

By now you've gained some valuable knowledge about what to do in order to be a successful networker; however, some of you may still be a bit hesitant to jump right in. In order to make this process more manageable (and less intimidating), the following are small steps you can take immediately to start seeing positive results. Once you've mastered the smaller steps, you will have the confidence to move forward toward your ultimate goals of having fun while networking, working less, and making more!

EIGHT HOT TIPS FOR CONNECTING TODAY

1. Step out of your comfort zone and meet one new person today. Be observant and focus on one positive quality that you admire in that individual. Compliment him or her on this quality and be a good listener. (Start with something small such as, "What a good-looking tie you have on—where did you get it from?)
2. Send a unique or humorous card along with a handwritten note to a person that you desire to connect with. (I can't stress enough the im-

portance of taking the time to write a personal greeting. In this hectic world we live in, people respond enthusiastically to someone who takes the time and effort to write a personal note. Remember to use these handwritten cards for your follow-up as well!)

3. Contact a good friend and ask for the name of the most friendly and outgoing person he or she knows—request a telephone number or address to either call or write that person.

4. Go to the library and look into the *Encyclopedia of Associations* (Detroit: Gale Research, 1996) for local groups you may have an interest in. (Another great source for locating this information is your local chamber of commerce.) Place a call to the top five groups and request that information be sent to you. Join the group that fits your needs.

5. Read your local newspaper and select an article about a person you'd like to know more about. Write a short note congratulating him or her on being in print. Enclose a business card and say you will be calling. In about a week, call. Remember to ask lots of questions—then let the person do the talking.

6. Make a list of everyone you currently know. Play matchmaker and see whom you can connect. Call each party and let him or her know what you are doing. Once a conversation between two parties has taken place, ask for feedback.

7. Go to a place or event where you normally wouldn't go (or wouldn't go alone) and smile at as many people as you can—make eye contact with them and then introduce yourself.

8. Sign up for a course. It can be for a hobby or business related—the point is to participate in activities with others who have common interests!

In order to take the work out of networking, you must first be aware of your current behaviors and beliefs. Only then can you replace them with new ways of conducting business and having fun doing it. If you still believe that meeting new people is painful, what do you think your networking results will be? However, if your belief about meeting new people is "I love learning about others and helping them," you will become a "people magnet," and you'll enjoy new relationships, increased business, and fun along the way. Networking isn't just a word to describe an action, it's a way of life—a way to stay connected to others.

Checklist for Moving On

	Yes	No
1. Do you understand and have you implemented the seven steps to creating good relationships?	____	____
2. Have you read *How to Win Friends and Influence Others*?	____	____
3. Do you see the value of "promoting others first," and have you taken the initiative to do so?	____	____
4. Have you prepared a list of people you currently know and contacted them?	____	____
5. Did you make a list of individuals who will be a part of your "sales team"?	____	____
6. Have you acted on any of the "Hot Tips for Connecting Today"?	____	____

► 9 ◄

Global Relationships

It's a Small World After All

You gain strength, courage, and confidence
by every experience in which you really stop to look fear
in the face. . . . You must do the thing you cannot do.
Eleanor Roosevelt

Never before has it been easier to gain access to the entire world!
Through satellites, computers, telephones, and faxes, we now have
the ability to communicate with our brothers and sisters abroad. So
why does it seem so overwhelming? And why should we be interested
in faraway places that we may never visit or that might not seem to
affect our own little world?

Whether you realize it or not, *unless we engage in peaceful global relations, we cannot exist peacefully ourselves.* If there is a war going on in
the Persian Gulf, does it affect your day-to-day life? Yes! And not
only for those families or persons in the armed forces. These struggles
engage us all on some level, whether it's personal, financial, in the
workplace, or elsewhere. At first glance, these struggles may not seem
to affect your day-to-day life, but ultimately they will. So what can
you do to improve diverse relations in your own community, company, or life? We can begin by understanding diversity (rather than
opposing it) and by realizing that working together can produce win-
win situations.

Understanding Cultural Diversity in the Workplace

Many individuals resent diversity in the workplace because it is forced on them. We resist change because it's different and uncomfortable, especially if we feel that we do not have a choice. Most people faced with communicating with diverse groups of people focus on the differences before looking at the things that are held in common. Often, *not being able to get past the differences prevents us from even looking at the commonalities and the possibility of building relationships that work well*. Before we can assume different beliefs that might serve us better, we must learn to understand our beliefs about diverse cultures.

Stereotypes, although often wrong, can hold some truth. Unfortunately, most stereotypes focus on the negative aspects of a culture. These stereotypes may unknowingly become part of our belief system. Whether we derive our beliefs from our parents, friends, or society in general, many times they are based on others' opinions of different cultures rather than our own opinions. When we engage in buying into other people's beliefs, we deprive ourselves of ever getting to know diverse cultures and developing our own beliefs.

Ask yourself now what your beliefs are about different cultures? Do you believe that all black people look the same? If so, you've probably never allowed yourself to "see" how unique each person is. Do you believe that all men who live in Italy pinch women as they walk down the street? Do you believe that all Russian women have mustaches and are large and unattractive? Many of these beliefs are perpetuated in our society by the movies, the media, and people's narrow view of the world.

Are you open to a new way of thinking? Are you willing to consider each human being as one with unique and special qualities? Or are you going to continue to buy into negative stereotypes?

Opening Up Your World

Once you determine that you are open-minded enough to consider each person from different cultures individually, you can ask yourself how you came to some of your beliefs. Did you meet a person from Germany who seemed rather cool? Did you assume that all people from Germany must be aloof? Are you open to understanding that perhaps it was just one person's demeanor that made you believe this way? Are you open to considering that being reserved may be part of the German culture as a sign of respect, and this in no way determines that the culture is unfriendly? These thought-provoking questions can be used to help you understand your beliefs about all cultures and races.

In order to get to know how we are similar (which is the fundamental tool for building solid relationships), let's examine some cultural differences and learn how to accept and honor these differences. Once we embrace these differences, we can make a plan to overcome the obstacles to engaging in productive global relationships.

Recognizing and Understanding Our Differences

According to George Dunn, a cultural anthropologist who has studied diversity training for many years, one of the first steps in identifying differences is to listen carefully and ask the right questions. You can choose to focus on how people of different cultures feel about moral values, gender roles, and work ethics. In other words, educate yourself on the differences and use your knowledge of them as an opportunity to build productive relationships.

For example, many Japanese individuals place a great deal of importance on agreements. Americans often make agreements casually and then do not hold to the original agreement. (See more about making agreements in Chapter 3). This cultural difference can lead to a misunderstanding (refusing to acknowledge a different style) that could be insulting to the other party and ruin a relationship immediately.

Language can also be a barrier to full understanding between people of different cultures. Don't assume that people of any culture immediately understand you because you speak the same language. Words often have several meanings, and to avoid misunderstandings, it's important to clarify what is understood by both parties. (Read more about communicating for better success in Chapter 6). When you say something, ask for feedback. Say, "What is your understanding about what I just communicated?" If the party responds with something different from what you intended, think of another way to state your question or response that may help them to understand you better. Don't talk louder! Often when people don't understand us, we tend to say the same thing more loudly. This only creates tension. Instead ask, "How can I clarify myself so that I can help you to better understand what I am saying?" By responding with the emphasis on

"I" rather than on "you," you'll create trust instead of defensiveness. Do not say, "You don't understand! How can you better understand what I am saying?" which places all the responsibility on the other party, who probably already feels intimidated. *Make it easier for others, and it will be easier for you!*

Another way to understand differences between cultures is to see how other cultures live. If you can't visit a certain country, start by going to restaurants featuring this culture's cuisine. You can learn a great deal about people by the food they eat, the entertainment they enjoy, and the company they keep. If you desire to learn more about the Mexican or Latin culture, attend a Cinco de Mayo parade in your area or go to a museum that focuses on these cultures.

Remember the old saying, "when in Rome do as the Romans do"? The same applies throughout the world. The following are a few tips to keep in mind while conducting business abroad:

When in England, men shouldn't wear striped ties while doing business because they connote different British regiments.

If using business cards in Taiwan, one side should be printed in English and the other in Mandarin.

In India, China, and Japan, self-driving by foreigners isn't permitted. Therefore, foreigners must hire a car and driver.

Most businesses in Chile are—or once were—family owned. Having family connections, an agent, or a local contact initiate a meeting is a must.

In the Los Angeles area alone there are over 150 languages spoken besides English! This can cause some major problems. What are some of the solutions? Once we recognize differences, we must then look for the things we have in common. (See Chapter 8 on building relationships.)

Recognizing Our Similarities

Mr. Dunn suggests that one facet all cultures have in common is that *we are all motivated by the desire to improve the quality of our personal lives.* In addition, many individuals are seeking to improve the quality of other people's lives as well. When we look at what we all have in common and use that as the core of building a good relationship (intentions = results), we discover we really aren't so different after all. After we get past the language barrier, and that difference of skin colors or the way we live, we might discover very similar desires; then we can build successful relationships.

Take some time now to think about the people in your life who come from a different culture. If you don't have anyone in your life who is different, ask yourself why? When you think about letting different cultures be a part of your life, do you feel fearful? If so, it may be because we often fear what we do not know. Are you willing to get past the fear? Are you willing to become interested in learning about different cultures? If your answer is no, why not? Do you tell yourself it's because you don't have the time? Or is it because you just don't care about it? Remember, one of the 25 qualities of successful people is curiosity. Curious people choose to know and learn about all aspects of life they haven't experienced, and they are typically more successful than people who don't.

Once you have developed a healthy curiosity, you can then begin to look for the commonalities we all share:

1. Love. Every human being has the desire to love and be loved (whether they express this desire or not).
2. Faith. This is a belief in a higher being or purpose to life (whether it's Buddha, God, Jesus, etc.).
3. Tradition. Each culture has traditions, passed on from generation to generation, that give them joy and comfort.
4. Creation and death. Every culture has the ability to give birth and every human being dies.
5. Change. Every culture goes through change.
6. Feelings. Each and every human has emotions; we all laugh, cry, and get angry.

As you can see, the qualities we have in common are those qualities that are most important to all human beings. Are we so different after all? It seems to me that other than the appearance of our bodies, where we live, and the language we use, we are exactly the same. The next time you meet someone from another culture look for the similarities. *You will always see what you look for!*

How You Can Effect Global Change and Understanding

You've heard the saying "It starts with only one person," and this applies to you! You don't have to assume the role of Rosa Parks, who spurred on an entire civil rights movement; however, you can start effecting change within your own home, community, and organization.

If you do not have any culturally diverse people in your life, go out and meet them! If you currently do have diverse relationships, expand them more fully. If you don't have any programs in your company, industry, or organization, start one. If you do have ongoing cultural diversity programs in your company, get involved to improve them. Don't let the corporate decision makers decide on what's right for your environment. If you believe you can improve cultural relationships, by all means get involved.

The Benefits You'll Receive from Participating in Diverse Relationships

Many people still don't understand the tremendous benefits to broadening their horizons by including diverse cultures in their immediate world. Let's explore some of them:

1. Economic. Building global relationships can increase your value (and that of your product and service) to millions of people. Therefore, you can anticipate additional revenue.
2. Satisfaction. A sense of deep fulfillment is achieved when we explore and develop relationships with other cultures.
3. Knowledge. An interest in and working toward building relations with other cultures leads to a better understanding of ourselves, and to continuous lifelong learning. Knowledge is power in any language!

I can speak firsthand about the opportunities and benefits of understanding and developing diverse cultural relationships. My first experience in dealing with another culture was when I began my career as a recruiter. I was engaged by a Japanese client to search for an addition to his office staff. He was very courteous and specific in his request. Initially I had some trouble understanding him verbally, but through persistence and careful feedback, I was able to determine what his desires were. I learned that this client was skeptical about dealing with an agency, and we had not had the opportunity to build trust by having a face-to-face meeting. In order to start building that trust, I decided to let him know how much I appreciated the opportunity to service his organization.

My mom used to raise small-planter-size bonsai. I proceeded to contact several florists in the area to locate a bonsai to send to my client. After several attempts, I located one and arranged to have it delivered to him. The response I received was worth the effort. Not only was my client extremely pleased, he went on to hire many more of his office staff through me. The small investment I made in that tree brought me a 1,000% return. However, I didn't do it for the money. I truly understood that this man was new to America and felt out of his comfort zone. I wondered how I could build a relationship of trust with him so I could better service him and at the same time wanted to give him a little "piece of home." (I've since learned the importance the Japanese culture places on gift-giving.)

Another Japanese client I recruited for gave me an opportunity to teach him something. This hiring official insisted that I send him a person over the age of 40. He explained that he wanted a woman far past the childbearing years so that children wouldn't interfere with her work. Rather than get angry, at his blatant discrimination and not work with this client, I believed that I could educate him. First, I explained that in America we were not allowed by law to discriminate against people because of age. I assured him that I understood what he really wanted was loyalty and maturity rather than just age. I further explained that I knew 20-year-old individuals who were very mature and 40-year-olds who were irresponsible. Would he prefer that I look more for maturity and dependability over age? He agreed. I also offered to send him three people, all of different ages and maturity levels, to interview. After his interviews he selected, surprisingly, the youngest of the three. I am happy to report that Joanne stayed with him for over 10 years, she had two children during this time, and my client was quite pleased with her tenure. We can teach different cultures, and they in turn can teach us. It is a two-way street, and all parties have a great deal to offer one another.

Focusing On the Solutions, Not the Problems

George Dunn has implemented the following summarized solutions to developing solid culturally diverse relationships:

1. Listen.
2. Understand.
3. Reserve judgment.
4. Consciously reject stereotypes.
5. Share your own cultural point of view. Share your life with others.

In addition, you could take a foreign language class or a course on diversity, or subscribe to a culturally diverse newspaper or magazine (have it translated if you don't know the language). A terrific newsletter that addresses many of the issues we have spoken of is *Cultural Diversity at Work: Preparing You for Managing, Training, and Conducting Business in the Global Age* (Seattle: GilDeane Group). For international business protocol, *The Diplomat* newsletter can help you decipher the proper customs for successfully conducting business in foreign places.

When all else fails, SMILE; everyone understands a smile.

Checklist for Moving On

	Yes	No
1. Did you take a look at your beliefs about different cultures?	___	___
2. Have you faced the fact that stereotypes can lead to misunderstandings?	___	___
3. Have you taken the time to seek out people of different cultures and to notice the differences and similarities?	___	___
4. Have you read a foreign paper, asked questions of people of different cultures, or taken a class to make strides toward greater understanding?	___	___
5. Have you focused on solutions rather than problems?	___	___

Prospering by Seeing the Big Picture and Putting the Pieces Together

I've been rich and I've been poor; rich is better.
Sophie Tucker Singer

What does prosperity mean? To prosper, according to *Websters II New Riverside Dictionary*, means "*to flourish, succeed, thrive, or experience favorable results.*" There was a time when America was deemed the place to come, where you could live your dream and get rich. Why then are many Americans a paycheck away from being homeless? Why does it appear that many individuals live from paycheck to paycheck? Why do so many people lack good health, healthy relationships, and peace of mind?

Are You Living in a World of Lack or Prosperity?

There was a time when I became financially destitute. I thought, "How could this happen to me?" Going bankrupt only happened to others, right? Wrong! Millions of Americans are filing bankruptcy at an alarming rate. Once again, I ask you, "How could this happen in a rich country like the United States?"

Early in my career I earned a substantial amount of money. I got married, bought a home (nothing extraordinary, but nice nonetheless), had two luxury automobiles, a nice wardrobe, and so on. I was living the American dream. After my divorce, I attempted to continue in the lifestyle I was accustomed to. I was able to manage doing that for a couple of years until a semirecession hit my industry. Rather than limit my spending, I relied on credit cards and financing to fill in the gaps. It soon caught up with me. I was in over my head and couldn't see any way out, so I chose to file bankruptcy.

I was humiliated beyond words. I was embarrassed to tell my friends and family, and I lived a life of secrecy. When I went to work for Kathleen (the woman who taught me to have more fun in business), she explained how I got into my predicament. She told me that I was "living from lack." I was deeply offended and angrily told her how wrong she was. Kathleen pointed out to me that I didn't believe I was worthy of being financially rich. Well, it's hard to ignore a person who's right, especially one who had money to burn. It was a difficult pill to swallow, but I put aside my pride and decided to learn what she and others obviously knew—the secret of wealth!

The Secret of Wealth

I became intrigued with how the rich got to be rich. I read many books on the subject and found one common theme throughout. *Prosperous people believe they deserve all the finest that life has to offer!* When I examined my own beliefs about money, I discovered that Kathleen was indeed correct.

I recall that as a young girl, my grandmother worked as a companion to a wealthy elderly man. He owned several mansions and traveled throughout the world in a luxurious fashion. He was also extremely generous and treated my grandmother and her family as part of his. I traveled to his winter home in Palm Springs, California, lived among celebrities, rode in Mercedes, and tagged along to four-star restaurants. When I look back at the experience, I guess my beliefs about money were being formed. I lived on the outskirts of money. My family was not wealthy; we were middle class. Money was for other people. Of course, I didn't realize I felt this way about money. I always strived to get it even though, deep down, I never truly believed I would be wealthy. One belief I can still recall I attribute to my grandmother who said frequently, "See those mansions, those are houses not homes. You live in a happy home—they live in houses." My grandmother's intentions were not to deter me from becoming wealthy but were instead an attempt to make me "feel better" about where I lived. Her own dismay at not being able to provide for us in the way she desired manifested itself in statements to us that helped us to believe money was not such a good thing. The following list will help you define your beliefs regarding prosperity:

What Are Your Beliefs about Prosperity?

1. How much money do you desire to have?
2. Do you believe you have to "work hard" to be wealthy?
3. How much do you believe you are worth?
4. What would you do today if you had $1 million?
5. Do you enjoy paying your bills?
6. Are you financially independent?
7. Do you believe money is "the root of all evil"?
8. Would you feel guilty about being rich?
9. Do you believe that by sacrificing wealth you are a more spiritual person?
10. Do you believe that people who are financially rich are unhappy?

In her book *The Dynamic Laws of Prosperity* (Marina del Rey, CA: De-Vorss Publications, 1985), Catherine Ponder recounts how her dismal financial circumstances led her to discover that the *power of thought can be used as an instrument for success or failure*. She came to realize that her failure was the result of her "failure thinking." Once she learned to better use her mind, she grasped the wonderful success secret and the tide began to turn! Ms. Ponder goes on to explain that "You are prosperous to the degree that you are experiencing peace, health, and plenty in your world." Prosperity consciousness is not only about money. Rather, it is about being committed to enjoying all the rewards of life: good health, happy relationships, financial independence, and fulfillment of your life's desires.

In Tod Barnhart's book, *The Five Rituals of Wealth* (New York: HarperCollins, 1995), he suggests that because of "dream traps," people drastically fail to achieve financial independence. The first trap is failure to make wealth a priority by responsibly managing the resources we already possess. The second is failure to find lifework that expresses our best self and creates total abundance. The third is failure to set goals and plan for our financial future. The fourth is failure to let the free enterprise system work for us and our money. And the fifth is failure to use our money as a tool to create value for ourselves and others.

Assuming New Beliefs about Prosperity

As you can see there is a theme to this entire book. The theme is that *our thoughts create our reality.* In order to change our current status, we must first understand our beliefs about prosperity and then make a commitment to engaging new beliefs that will bring us the results we desire.

Once I understood how "lack" was affecting my life, I experienced a dramatic turn of events. I was able to direct my energy toward giving myself permission to attracting money easily and frequently. At the time I began learning about prosperity, after my bankruptcy and the loss of my home, I committed to a new way of life. I made a firm decision that I *was worthy of following my dream and having the money to make it a reality.*

Soon after I practiced this affirmation, I met a man, through a friend, who offered me an apartment. I resisted his suggestion and explained that I had no money to pay for it. He told me that I could get this apartment on a barter exchange. In exchange for my services of recruiting and career counseling, I could pay for the apartment. I was thrilled. Was this legal? "Of course," he said. "It works just like money, and you pay taxes on it to boot!" He agreed to let me go into the negative balance for one year's rent, saying he trusted me to pay it back.

Of course I was excited but suspicious as well. Here was a perfect stranger offering me a deal too good to be true. However, I remembered my affirmation, I believed I was worthy of this good fortune, and proceeded to make my dream into a reality! There was only one catch. I had to pay the security deposit in cash. At the time, I had about $100 to my name and was already in debt to my family and friends. However, I decided that opportunity was knocking, and I had better answer. So I did what any other person who had passion, desire, and commitment would have done—I took a risk.

A friend of mine knew a man who was quite wealthy. She suggested that I call him and ask him for the money. I begged her to do it for me, but she felt funny about it. Rather than jeopardize my friendship with her, I decided to call him myself. I don't have the words to describe how I felt before I picked up the phone. I kept repeating my affirmation until I had the courage to dial. When he answered the phone, I explained who I was and why I was calling. I said, "I know you don't know me, but I am a friend of a friend and I need your help." I went on to tell him my circumstances and that I was asking for his trust even though I was a perfect stranger. I promised him I would pay him back, with interest, in one month. He hesitantly agreed. I kept my word and even paid him back early. Several years later, he became my silent partner on my first book deal!

Taking Action on Your New Beliefs

None of this would have happened if I hadn't been willing to ask for help and hold firmly to my new beliefs. Once you begin thinking differently, you'll start behaving differently! One of the actions that create a more prosperous lifestyle is to *learn to pay yourself*. This was a great challenge to me. I was accustomed to paying my bills first, and whatever was leftover was what I would keep—except nothing was ever leftover! I began to keep a log of the money I earned. I took 10% of the money to pay myself, and took the second 10% to tithe to sources from which I received spiritual growth.

My financial status began to improve immediately! Soon, however, I began to fall back into my old ways. I gave up paying myself and just concentrated on tithing. I guess at the time I still believed that giving my money away was more noble than paying myself. My income dropped off a bit. I was still doing better than before, though, and I didn't mind that I couldn't get some of the things I desired. Then when I finally realized I was putting others first, again, I was able to go back to paying myself first.

As Tod Barnhart states in his five dream traps, "failure to finding one's lifework to express our best self" is a key factor in coming from lack. You must *believe you have a purpose and pursue your special talents in order to become prosperous!* Take a tiny step today toward fulfilling your purpose and pursuing your lifework.

So far you've learned to assume new beliefs, to practice affirming statements, and to pay yourself first! The next step is to make your money work for you!

Making Your Money Work for You

Barnhart asks people the age-old question, "If I were your fairy godmother, which of these two wishes would you rather I grant you: a million dollars cash right now, or a magic penny that doubles itself every day?" He suggests that most people would opt for the cash upfront; however, the far wiser choice is the magic penny. Why? The magic penny would be worth well over $1 trillion by day 45!

The second biggest challenge for me was to let go of the belief that girls don't do well in math and finance. I still don't love to read about finance; however, I choose to understand the financial marketplace. You can, too. In other words, get to know about stocks, bonds, and mutual funds. Request assistance from a financial planner to help educate you on your choices. Read books. Some great books on assuming a prosperity consciousness are The Instant Millionaire: A Tale of Wisdom and Wealth by Mark Fisher (Novato, CA: New World Library, 1990); The Richest Man in Babylon by George S. Clason (New York: Penguin, 1955); Do What You Love, the Money Will Follow by Marsha Sinetar (New York: Paulist Press, 1986); and Wealth 101 by John Roger (Los Angeles: Prelude Press, 1992).

Another common thread among successful individuals is their belief that a higher power guides them. In the past, discussing one's spiritual beliefs was frowned upon in corporate life. However, I believe the tide is indeed turning. More and more people are "coming out of the closet" and relaying personal stories about their faith. So how do we stay centered in our spiritual beliefs without offending others?

How Your Spiritual Beliefs Affect Your Lifework

When I began my business career in 1977, I was naive to people's different faiths. I recall sitting in the lunchroom on break one day and asking a young woman when her birthday was. She replied that she had no birthday. I was confused and said, "Everyone has a birthday!" She explained that she was a Jehovah's Witness and that they didn't celebrate birthdays. "So," I said, "It's not that you don't have a birthday, it's just that you don't celebrate it!" (I admit I was very invested in being right, not happy!) She angrily got up and stormed out of the lunchroom. I was both surprised and hurt. "What did I do?" I exclaimed to my coworkers. I had never heard of this religious group, and this belief went against those I had grown up with. I learned that day never to discuss religion on the job. (Over the years I added politics, sex, and money to that list as well.)

Religion versus Spirituality

Religion is a specific unified system of belief whereas spirituality is relating to or having the nature of spirit (or soul). In my experience, people who are "religious" believe solely in their chosen denomination as the best way to know their creator whereas "spiritual" individuals believe there are many ways to know one's higher power. They believe it doesn't matter what road you travel to find your God; as long as you stay on the road, you will be rewarded.

My belief is we can't love God as fully as he intended us to if we live in fear. Many religious leaders are adamant about putting a stop to this "New Age Thinking" because they feel it is detrimental and will corrupt those with weak values. I've attended several places of worship where the religious leaders have spoken of this "New Age Way" and how fearful they are of the outcome.

God is Love

No matter what your belief about God, God is love! No matter what name you give your higher power, whether it is Buddha, God, or Jesus Christ, love is the common bond. When love exists in our hearts, there cannot be fear. It is my opinion that when we fear, we turn our souls away from the light of God (or our higher power).

Why then, are we so opposed to talking about the one source of power and love we are all created from? Unfortunately, as we discussed in Chapter 9, when we have different beliefs, we often tend to shut out those who think and believe differently.

It is my belief that we are all right. Religion or spirituality is a personal belief not to be inflicted on others but to be shared for a common understanding of universal love. I didn't always believe this way, but through my life experiences I have come to a new understanding.

Fear of God

I was raised Presbyterian and went to church regularly as a young girl, until about the age of ten. During this time I went to church because

I had to, not because I wanted to. I was actually afraid of our minister! He spoke loudly and yelled often (most likely to wake the people who were asleep in the back pews!). I was taught to fear the wrath of God. To a small child, this is not only scary but can result in an unhealthy relationship with God!

When my parents got divorced, we stopped attending church altogether, and by the time I was a teenager, I had developed a passive relationship with God. I received little or no direction on dealing with death, adversity, or crisis and turned away from God completely. As a young adult, I became angry with God (how could he let so many bad things happen to me and others?), and somewhere along the way I made a decision to not include God in my life. Without faith, my life became centered around self-gratification. My 20s were consumed with accumulation of material wealth and status symbols. By the time I reached my late 20s, I was a mess!

Learning to Love Again

We often "find God" again when our lives fall apart. With no one to turn to, feeling helpless and hopeless, I began to search for some meaning to my life. Through the personal growth courses I attended, where I learned to let go of my anger, I was able to entertain the idea of a "higher power." I started talking with others about their spiritual beliefs, began reading books, and attending church again. I explored every avenue I could to find answers to my never-ending questions of "Why?"

After learning to forgive myself and to let go of the shame and anger that bound me to misery for such a long time, I was able to learn to love again—even to love God! Then I quit struggling and learned to allow my life to "flow" according to my best and highest purpose. I found both peace of mind and a sense of self that allowed me to fulfill my lifework.

Integrating Faith and Spirituality in Your Life and Work Environment

About three years ago, I sat at a table in a crowded Chicago restaurant with several prominent businesswomen. One woman published a major fashion magazine, another was a top image consultant, and the third was the author of a highly praised business book. I admired each woman for her accomplishments; however, I felt distant from our conversation—we were "talking business"—until I overheard one of the women explaining how visualization had changed her life. My ears perked up, and I asked about her beliefs. Immediately the conversation turned toward spirituality in the workplace, and we each shared our common experiences of what God meant in our lives. It was a lively luncheon, and we became excited about the prospect of the "changing world of work." The fact that we felt comfortable sharing our thoughts about God, miracles, angels, and the like, was astonishing to all of us; only a few short years before, none of us would have dared broach such a controversial subject!

Since that day, I have assumed a new attitude about sharing my thoughts and beliefs, and I now have a sign on my desk that reads, "God is my Partner." I rely heavily on him for all my business decisions and ask for his guidance in every step I take. If I forget this partnership (which I sometimes do), I am gently reminded by a situation or phone call that brings it to my attention again.

Recently, when my mother became ill, I felt the "old struggle" with fear surface again. I wanted to be able to take off as much time as I could to be with her; however, being in business for oneself requires that one work to get paid. My sister and brother both worked for companies that gave them paid personal leave and, therefore, were under no financial strain. I was pleased that they had bosses who were so understanding, and I wished that I had a boss to turn to for a paid leave. Suddenly it dawned on me! I did. I turned to my partner (God) and said, "God, I would like to have all the time necessary to spend with my mom and still get paid for it." As soon as I turned my struggle over to him, I was free of any negativity and proceeded to fly out to be with Mom.

I took a total of one month off. When I returned I was faced with the deadline for this book (which was creeping up on me quickly) and mounting bills. I continued my prosperity affirmations, and within days, I began to see results. I received a deposit refund check from a book warehouse I had used over four years ago (I almost threw it out because I thought it was junk mail!); I found a check in an envelope of old photos that was never cashed; I got a consulting assignment that paid me a retainer; and the list goes on. In other words, God had granted my request—I had indeed received my paid personal leave!

Trusting Your Intuition at Work

Those of you who work for conservative corporate cultures may feel inhibited about sharing your views on faith. You may feel that you could lose your job as a result of your beliefs. *I can assure you that if you lose your job because of your faith in God or your higher power, you are required elsewhere.* Now, I'm not suggesting you go out and get a megaphone to announce your beliefs or force them on others. What I am saying is that you have a right to use your faith in making any life decision whether you are at home or at work. When we follow our intuition (which I believe is our voice connected to God), we can't go wrong! When I began to use my intuition more often, I noticed my business life flowed easily. If I avoided listening to my inner-voice, I was often stressed, frustrated, and upset.

How can we each get in touch with our intuition? Laura Day's book *Practical Intuition* (New York: Villard Books, 1996) deals with tapping into our own inner guide. One simple theme to remember has to do with the importance of asking the right questions. Have you ever heard the expression "Garbage in, garbage out"? Intuition works sort of the same way. If you've ever watched Barbara Walters interview someone, did you notice how she has a way of drawing out information or emotions? She's a master at asking questions that will provide answers with clear meanings. In other words, she avoids "garbage out" because her questions are purposeful and well-composed.

Successful people in many fields have developed their skills as interviewers. They use the same skills to question themselves as they would to ask questions of an expert witness or a major client. They use questions whose answers will provide clear direction to the next step. The next time you desire to tap into you intuition, ask yourself (1) What exact information am I looking for? and (2) Are my beliefs and expectations blocking me from accessing my inner-voice? Allow this information to appear at the right time—when it is for your best and highest good. When you are truly open to your intuition, not only will the answers come to you, but you'll also have a good feeling and motivation for taking the next step.

Before writing this book, I was writing a book to educate employers on how to recruit and hire effectively. I wrote three chapters before noticing how difficult the project had become. I got resistance from everyone I interviewed; the surveys I designed and sent out were never returned; and, all in all, the project was not a lot of fun! One day while taking a shower (I get some of my best ideas in the shower!), a light bulb went on, and I realized that I no longer chose to continue writing the book. I got the distinct message to write an alto-gether different kind of book.

Well, my logic told me that giving up the hiring book was silly. How could I throw all my hard work away? But the thought of a dif-ferent kind of book excited me. That morning I put aside my hiring notes and began instead to tap into my thoughts on this book. Within a few days, I had developed an outline and the result is what you are now reading. I had complete faith in knowing that this project would be fun, challenging, and right for me. Even when publisher after pub-lisher turned it down, I held strongly to the belief that I must write this book.

There was a point when, after a year of rejection, I felt that per-haps I had made an error in listening to my intuition. Maybe I had heard it wrong? I contemplated giving up the idea of writing and in-stead get a "real job." For approximately one month I struggled with the thought of giving up. During this time, through the support of my life coaches and meditations, I asked for direction. Time and again I was directed back to the question "What do you choose to have?" When the thought of losing this project looked real to me, I gained the insight that I truly desired to write this book. Two weeks later my agent called with a publisher! Sometimes, it's necessary to be re-minded of how much we desire something before we are willing to recommit to it 100%.

Using the Golden Rule at Work

How simple a concept and how powerful it is: "Do unto others as you would have them do unto you." If you are not working for an organi-zation that supports this rule, you will most definitely not have peace of mind. But just because your company does not adhere to this phi-losophy doesn't necessarily mean you must quit. Sometimes you find yourself in the role of teacher. It starts by taking a risk and not giving in when you know what others are doing is wrong.

About 10 years ago, I worked for a recruitment agency that lacked both integrity and moral values. The owner wanted me to lie to a client about a fee, which in turn would cause me to lie to the job seeker. I felt like I needed this job. I was a single mom with two small children, and the thought of losing a substantial fee and my job was awful. However, I knew myself and I didn't think I could sleep at night if I lied about this. I confronted my boss by telling him I couldn't lie and I wanted to make another arrangement—I would take a smaller fee, rather than lie. I would not have wanted someone to lie to me, and so I followed the Golden Rule.

My boss was not pleased but he agreed, and I took the lesser fee. Several months later he fired me! Yes, I survived. No, it wasn't a pleasant experience; however, I had the satisfaction of not selling out, and I slept very well. This owner has since gone out of business, and the last I heard, he was in financial ruin and quite unhappy. I hope he has learned, as I have, that "what goes around in life, comes around." In addition to using your faith and intuition in your business life, balancing the two at home is just as important!

Living Your Faith in Your Personal Life

There was a time after I turned my life over to God, in order to allow it to flow according to my best and highest good, when situations would occur that tested my faith down to its very core! I remember one in particular. For 10 years, I had raised my daughters with great pride and love. When my oldest daughter decided to go live with her dad, I thought my world had fallen apart, and I questioned God extensively on this occurrence.

I believed it was not for either my daughter's or my own highest good that she live with her father. I cried, yelled, and literally became physically ill during this time. I felt stripped of my identity as a mother and was concerned about what other people would think of me. I thought people would judge me as being an unfit mother. Why else would she choose to go live with her dad? I was miserable. As time went by, I began to realize (once again), how we don't have the capacity as human beings to fully understand the actions of God. When I was able to disengage from my ego (which I understand is short for Edging God Out), I began to relax and let my life flow again.

I've come to understand that we won't always know the reasons behind his decisions, and the true meaning of faith requires us to be nonjudgmental and to keep in our minds, hearts, and souls that God knows what's best for us. This is the challenge we all face: *we must learn to be thankful not only for the good times but for the painful ones as well.* My daughter and I now have a much deeper and more satisfying relationship than ever before; I doubt this could have happened without her moving to her father's home.

Counting Your Blessings

Whenever I begin to stray and slip into feeling sorry for myself (which happens occasionally although much less frequently than ever before), I remind myself to count my blessings. I write out a list of things for which I am thankful. I recommend engaging in this exercise often, even when you are feeling joyful. It is a wonderful way to be with God often, and it uplifts your spirit.

When I first began writing down my blessings, I sometimes had trouble even coming up with one or two things. After all, I was bankrupt and homeless—I could barely find any blessing in this! However, I focused on the fact that I had my health, two beautiful children, caring friends, and life! If nothing else, sometimes the fact that we are alive and breathing can be all the inspiration necessary to get motivated.

What I've found over the past 10 years is that God desires for us to have it all: peace of mind, wealth, health, and happiness. He isn't the one who stands in our way of having heaven on earth—*we are.* Do yourself a favor; get out of your own way and surrender to your higher power. You'll find, as millions of us have, that this can be the best thing you ever did for yourself and for others!

Checklist for Moving On

	Yes	No
1. Did you take the quiz on prosperity beliefs?	___	___
2. Have you discovered new beliefs on living prosperously?	___	___
3. Have you taken action steps based on these new beliefs?	___	___
4. Did you plan a way for your money to make more for you?	___	___

(continued)

Checklist (*continued*)

	Yes	No
5. Have you considered how your spiritual beliefs affect your lifework?	——	——
6. Have you given thought to partnering with your "higher power"?	——	——
7. Did you practice using your intuition?	——	——
8. Do you use the Golden Rule at work and at home?	——	——
9. Have you turned your life over to your "higher power"?	——	——
10. Did you take time to count your blessings?	——	——

▶ *11* ◀

Making a Difference Out There

There are two ways of spreading light;
to be the candle or the mirror that reflects it.
Edith Wharton

Why "If It's Meant to Be, It's Up to Me"

I sat there staring at the television in horror. I had just learned that a child, the third that week, had fallen more than twenty floors in an inner-city housing project and was dead. I blinked back my tears and thought of my own sweet children—how fortunate I was that they were alive. Then I got angry! Why was this happening? These poor, helpless children with no safe place to play were being killed for no reason. "Why doesn't someone do something?" I shouted at the television. No one answered. I sat alone for a few more minutes when suddenly I laughed (not a ha-ha laugh but a sad, ironic laugh). Here I was waiting for someone else to do something. Why not me? Everyone was waiting around for "someone else." Sadly, so was I.

I made a decision to do it differently. The following morning I called the Chicago Housing Authority and spoke to the woman in charge of erecting window guards that would prevent these occurrences. She explained that the work was going slowly because the individuals installing the window guards often quit because they were getting shot at. Also, the funds that were allocated for the window guards might be used to buy fuel for the winter. I asked her what I could do to help. She suggested that money was what was needed. She informed me that each window unit cost $160.

I was excited. I told her that I knew many prominent business-people and I would do what I could to raise some money. Even if I raised only $1,600, I knew it could save at least 10 children's lives. I went to work. I drafted a letter explaining my mission and mailed out the letters to my closest friends and business associates. This was in July. By September, I had not heard a word from anyone. Not one check came in, nor any phone calls. "What gives . . . ?" I thought.

So, I telephoned each person I had sent the mailing to, and I asked about their lack of response. The comments I received were astonishing to me. "I'm not giving anything because I don't understand why the mothers don't watch their children. And why do they have the windows open at all?" "First of all," I explained, "many of the mothers are addicted to drugs, and the kids fend for themselves. Secondly, the children are stuck in buildings on the twentieth floor where they have no air-conditioning and the heat is over one hundred degrees. They have no safe place to play, and, besides, is it the children's fault?" "No," they responded. "However, I don't feel it's my fault either that people decide to live that way, and, besides, I already give money to another charity."

Call after call, the responses were the same. No one was concerned. My follow-up calls only resulted in people defending their reasons and feeling guilty. Around Christmastime I had a few checks roll in (most likely due to the feelings one gets around the holidays). I mailed in what little money I had gathered and apologized profusely to the public housing director for the lack of support. She said, "Don't feel bad, Vicki. Most people feel the same way. At least you saved a couple children. Feel good about that and the fact you actually took action." I agreed with her but hung up the phone feeling less than satisfied. I asked myself, "What is it going to take for people to get involved?" I realized then that it was part of my life's purpose to educate individuals like me to the benefits and results of volunteering.

With all the causes and charities these days, getting involved is rather overwhelming for most people. However, an organization called Citi Cares of America is making volunteerism easier for busy professionals. Whether it's time or money you decide to invest, it's your decision; however, the benefits of volunteering are so great you'll wonder why you never did it before, or why you don't do it more often!

Volunteering for a Better You and a Better World

Mary Prchal and Leslie Bluhm left the corporate world in 1991 to form Chicago Cares, Inc., an offshoot of Citi Cares of America. The mission of Citi Cares is to increase and promote a heightened understanding of community needs and community service, and to improve the quality of life in the communities served by Cares organizations.

"What makes Chicago Cares so unique," says Mary Prchal, co-founder, "is how easy we make volunteering for the busy professional. We call it 'no guilt' volunteering." Many people have considered volunteering, or have participated in programs in the past. However, many organizations desperate for volunteers keep hounding those who do participate until they no longer "feel good" about donating their time or money. These people are made to feel guilty by saying no to such a good cause. "By incorporating a 'no time commitment' policy at Chicago Cares, we have increased our volunteers to accommodate ninety different programs in the past five years," said Mary. "We offer a calendar of events with different programs and the volunteers choose what interests them or how much time they are willing to give—no hassle." The benefits to volunteering are incredible:

1. Access to a whole new experience and a variety of people.
2. A true sense of accomplishment.
3. Career enhancement.
4. Social opportunities.
5. Seeing the results of your participation within your community.

Ms. Prchal explains how gratifying volunteering can be. "Imagine working hard all day in corporate America and at night playing bingo with senior citizens. The change of pace is great and the smile you get in return is worth the little effort put in one hundred times over!" she says.

Two of the greatest benefits I have received from volunteering are a sense of accomplishment and the opportunity for new experiences

I might never have had otherwise. Several years ago, I was given the chance to participate in a program sponsored by the Chicago Housing Authority to clean up vacated apartments and donate them to the homeless in the community. These apartments were in terrible condition. Most had no heat, were filthy dirty, and were not fit to live in. Several of my friends and I donated our weekend to washing walls, painting, and general cleanup. When we arrived, we were escorted by security (it was not a safe environment because of gangs) to the building we were to work on. Faced with no running water, no heat, and less-than-safe circumstances, we were concerned but nonetheless determined to do the job we had set out to do. When all was said and done, we had managed to get five units ready for homeless families to occupy. Considering it was the dead of winter in Chicago, I was confident these families were thrilled not to have to sleep on the streets or in their cars. The personal gratification that gives me is something I would never give up.

Another benefit to volunteering is meeting new people with like-minded interests, especially if you're new to a city. Chicago Cares has a Social Time Out group that meets regularly for volunteers to get together and exchange stories. If you aren't willing to "go it alone," introduce a friend to a rewarding experience! If you decide to experience volunteering just for a day, cities across the country offer National Servathon Day, where corporate teams volunteer as well as individuals. Perhaps you'd just like to have the opportunity to make another person smile. That in itself can be reward enough!

Mary Prchal recalls one instance when a couple volunteered their services to be a big brother and sister to a young girl living in a home for abused and neglected children. Their attachment grew over time, and the couple ended up adopting her. If you volunteer from your heart, you never know how wonderfully it can impact your life.

The Pitfalls of Volunteering and How to Overcome Them

I must mention a very important aspect to successful volunteering. *Leave your expectations at home.* In corporate America, when we are assigned to a job, we are usually given all the tools to complete our assignments, or we have had similar experiences to relate to. This is not always so with volunteering. I had never even been within a mile of an inner-city housing development and had no idea what to expect.

In my case that served me well because then I was not intimidated or disappointed with my experience. I know several well-meaning people who were. They volunteered their time specifically to give back, but their expectations of "getting back" got in their way.

Take Sarah for example. Sarah is a good and caring person who used to volunteer often. These days, however, she isn't so inspired. Sarah explains that she thought she was helping by volunteering to teach a young man to read. Two and a half years after she began, he still didn't read any better than a first grader. Sarah says, "I admit I was frustrated. He just wasn't as dedicated to it as I was. So I gave up. And I felt lousy about the whole thing. Over two years of my life—for what?"

If you've ever experienced the frustrations of being let down over volunteering, you aren't alone. However, there are ways to overcome these challenges, and in order to have a successful volunteer experience, you may choose to assume a new attitude. The following are some qualities found in successful volunteers:

1. *They have no expectations. They give to the community without expecting something back.* This is easier said than done! It's a challenge to spend your time giving to someone or some group that may not appreciate it as much as you'd like. I recall a time when I was quite miffed because a group of hardworking people spent countless hours cleaning and planting a beautiful garden for an economically disadvantaged neighborhood only to find that across the street the sidewalks were lined with garbage! "Why should I care, if they don't?" was my response. I felt like I was more invested than they were. Once I changed my view of volunteering to include "no expectations," I was able to give freely. I decided to be happy instead of right.

2. *Successful volunteers are sensitive to the desires of others.* By respecting all people as equal and not "less fortunate," you can truly be sensitive to others' desires. You can't be a successful volunteer if you feel sorry for people or patronize them. It's important to remember that the only difference between you and them may be that, at this point in their life, they may not feel worthy and are coming from an attitude of lack. (See Chapter 10).

3. *Successful volunteers are leaders.* Volunteering is an opportunity to lead by example, to teach skills and attitudes others may not have been exposed to before. Chicago Cares offers volunteers the training they require to be successful. Like any other skill, volunteering takes commitment, time, and effort to make it a worthwhile venture for all. In addition, Chicago Cares also offers many corporate volunteer programs that can truly enhance your career.

Enhancing Your Career by Volunteering

When I speak to groups about *Getting Hired in the '90s,* many of the individuals attending are between career opportunities. I encourage them to volunteer for several reasons:

1. By becoming active in our community, we can meet many influential people (networking).
2. When we are between jobs, we often experience a need to feel useful. Volunteering fills that need (boosts self-esteem).
3. We can learn or improve leadership skills (experiences to add to your resume).
4. There may be an opportunity to explore not-for-profit programs (get informational interviews).
5. We may receive a job offer from other volunteers or participants.

Even if you work full-time, volunteering can enhance your career in many ways. Most larger corporations take part in volunteer programs. CEOs, as well as many other key decision makers, get involved. Often company newsletters or corporate publications dedicate articles to people in their firm who participate in volunteer events. These publications are read by the entire company (including CEOs), so when you volunteer, you can increase your visibility by getting companywide recognition.

Challenges Volunteer Organizations Face

Volunteering Is a Year-Round Need

It's Thanksgiving and the phone rings off the hook with volunteers ready and willing to donate their time to soup kitchens across the country. Often these volunteers are turned away because more people volunteer at the holidays than any other time of the year. During the dog days of summer, the food pantry's shelves are empty and volunteers are scarce. *Volunteers are needed all year-round, not just at the holidays!* If you only volunteer at Christmastime, make it your goal to do it differently this year.

The Gender Gap in Volunteering

Women make up 75% of all volunteers. Why is that? Are women better nurturers? Do they have more time on their hands? The answer is NO. Men are needed for a number of projects, and Citi Cares of America is responding to that need. They have developed many programs that interest men. With hundreds of programs to choose from, there is now no excuse for not lending a helping hand!

Volunteering Is for ALL Ages

Fifty percent of volunteers are in their 20s, 30% in their 30s. That leaves only 20% in all other age groups. In order to serve all the needs of our communities, it is up to all age groups to participate. In addition to gender-specific programs, Chicago Cares is considering adding opportunities for family volunteering. Not only will this encourage the youth of today to participate in creating a better future, it will give families the opportunity to share the experience. In this day and age when family values are at the forefront, consider making volunteering a family event!

Making Volunteerism Work in America

Citi Cares of America's brochure offers this insight: "Imagine if John Kennedy lived to see his challenge to *ask what you can do for your country* come to life in cities across America." Isn't it time that we give up the mentality of "what's in it for me?" and instead ask ourselves each and every day what we can do to give back? Without getting all patriotic on you, I suggest that when you write down your blessings (Chapter 10), if you live in America, add that to your list. We have it all here: freedom of speech (which I wholeheartedly endorse) and endless opportunities in a country founded by people just like us—individuals who truly decided to make America a better place to live!

Citi Cares of America's brochure suggests we look at those volunteers who tell their stories of making a difference through their actions: "If I'm only writing a twenty-five-dollar check out to an organization,

I'm not really making a difference . . . but by volunteering, it's exercise for the soul." *When was the last time you exercised your soul?* If it's been awhile, take that first step through the door of immense opportunity. I speak from experience when I say you'll be pleasantly surprised and rewarded hundreds of times over without ever expecting it!

Checklist for Moving On

	Yes	No
1. Have you decided on one thing you can do to make things different or better?	——	——
2. Do you understand the benefits you can receive from volunteering?	——	——
3. Have you taken steps to enhance your qualities and success as a volunteer?	——	——
4. Did you take action to get involved?	——	——

Troublesome feelings:

○ Anger : for being betrayed - doing what was right & being

Prefer anonymity - don't like dealing face to face w/ pax.

comfort zone:? ⌐ back to childhood?

Page

▶ *12* ◀

Shifting Sands in the Workplace

How to Change Careers and Industries without Missing a Stride

The only job you start out at the top on is digging a ditch.
William Ensley Carpenter

Do I Stay or Do I Leave?

Before you assume that your job is the reason for your unhappiness, it's important to define some of your troublesome feelings (anger, boredom, depression) and identify when they started. Was it a change of management? Did your spouse, a coworker, or a family member recently leave a job? Have you suffered a relationship breakup?

Frank worked for the family-owned business for 10 years. During that time he earned his MBA and felt underutilized in his position. Frustrated by his lack of upward mobility, he left his job and moved to another state. Six weeks into his new position, he found himself dealing with the very same issues that prompted his career change. His new boss treated him exactly the same way his father had in the family business. Frank was at a loss. How could he have been so wrong about making a job change? Had Frank identified his feelings of anger prior to leaving his dad's firm, he could have taken steps to solve these issues and then decided if a career change was truly in order.

Over the past 17 years of counseling individuals on job changes, I've found that we are often attracted to situations that recreate our _less confrontation_

— Being alone . —

comfort zone. These comfort zones stem from very early family experiences, and we many times try to recreate these experiences without even knowing it. Even though I had this awareness, it was still difficult to recognize this tendency in my own life. I personally recreated the same boss-employee relationships in five different jobs. These relationships were very similar to the one that I had with my father. Of course, had someone pointed that out to me at the time, I would have laughed and denied the similarity. However, upon reflection, I can now see why these relationships didn't work well.

Once I was able to deal with the feelings of anger regarding my father, I was able to heal myself enough to move to another level in my comfort zone. After that, I was no longer attracted to jobs that had similar boss-employee relationships. In fact, by identifying and resolving these conflicts, I developed the confidence to pursue starting my own company.

Take some time now to make a list of your feelings regarding your current position, boss, and coworkers. Do you see any similarities to when you were growing up? What qualities do your boss and coworkers have in common with your mom, dad, and siblings? (Refer to the section titled "Understanding How You Got to Where You Are (and Learning to Accept It!)" in Chapter 1.)

Is It Your Career—or Just Your Job?

Perhaps you've determined that it isn't your personal life that requires attention. Now you must decide if it's your job that is driving you crazy or your whole career. Many times it's the job, not the career. In order to find out where you are, complete the questionnaire from Chapter 4 ("Evaluation: Are You a 'Good Fit' for Your Current Position?"). Should you decide that your current job isn't what you want, you first must learn to "heal" the situation before moving on. Otherwise, like Frank, you're likely to recreate the same circumstances. If you take the actions necessary to resolve any past issues that may be affecting your current situation and you still feel unfulfilled, it's time to explore a making a career change.

Determining Your Desires

When you begin to explore all the possibilities and options available to you in the world, it can be quite overwhelming! It's important to learn to pay attention to clues that you may not have noticed before. Take a few moments to ask yourself the following questions: "What would I do for a living if money were not a factor? What if I only had six months left to live?" You may have decided you'd want to travel around the world. However, let's focus more on what you would do in a *career*. (Refer to Chapter 3: "Discovering Your Special Purpose".)

Next, revisit your childhood for a bit. What kind of activities and interests did you pursue as a young person? I always loved to read. When I look back at my youth, I can begin to see a pattern emerging. Besides enjoying books, I also loved to write papers. I especially enjoyed creative writing courses. In addition, I felt good about helping others and was often the "advice-giver" in my circle of friends. Not much has really changed over the years. However, now I am fulfilling these desires in a full-time career, and you can do the same. But first it takes knowing what you like and clearly understanding your desires. Books that may help you recognize your desires are *Live the Life You Love* by Barbara Sher (New York: Delacorte Press, 1996) and *The Artist's Way* by Julia Cameron (New York: Perigree Books, 1992).

Remember during this process to rely on your intuition. Even if it doesn't seem all that logical, pay attention to it as a clue to your next step in discovering what you truly want.

Assessing and Using Your Transferable Skills to Change Careers

After you've decided on a career to focus on, you must take an inventory of what skills and qualities you have to offer this career and what skills you must improve on to be successful at it. When I decided to write a book, I had no previous experience. I took an assessment of the qualities I already possessed and realized that I had very little experience in many of the skills necessary to be an accomplished writer. So, I went to work. The first quality I lacked was being self-disciplined enough to write on a schedule. Up to that point, I only wrote when I felt like it. With that system, it could have taken me an entire lifetime to complete my first book. I chose to make a change, so each and every day I set aside an hour to begin my writing. Many mornings I sat looking at an empty page for the entire hour. I was tempted to turn on *Oprah* and ignore my writing (I decided I could use her as inspiration) as I had done in the past. But I forced myself to begin a daily ritual of writing and developing some good habits.

From the following boxed list, circle the skills you currently possess, and with a highlighter, mark the skills you would like to improve on. (Refer also to the 25 entrepreneurial qualities in Chapter 4.)

Transferable Skills

act/perform	demonstrate	improve
advise people	design	improvise
analyze data	detail	inspect products
anticipate problems	determine	install
arrange functions	develop	instruct
assemble products	direct others	interview people
assess situations	dispense information	invent
audit records	distribute	inventory
bargain/barter	draft	investigate
budget money	edit	learn
build	enforce	learn quickly
buy products/services	entertain	liaison
calculate numbers	evaluate	listen
chart information	examine	locate information
check for accuracy	exhibit	logic
collect money	expedite	make/create
compare data	explain	make decisions
compile statistics	explore	make policy
compute data	file records	manage a business
conceptualize ideas	find information	manage people
control costs	fix/repair	mediate problems
control situations	follow directions	meet the public
converse with others	gather information	memorize
coordinate activities	guide/lead	information
cope with deadlines	hand-eye	mentor others
correspond	coordination	monitor progress
with others	handle	motivate others
create	complaints/money	negotiate
delegate maintenance	illustrate	nurse
deliver	imagine solutions	nurture

Transferable Skills (*continued*)

observe
operate equipment
order goods/supplies
organize people/
   tasks/data/
   meetings
own/operate business
paint
persuade others
plan
plant
prepare materials
print
process information
program

promote
question others
recruit people
reduce costs
refer people
remember
   information
research
resolve problems
run meetings
schedule
sell
service customers
service equipment
set goals/objectives

set up systems
sew
sketch
socialize
solve problems
speak in public
study
supervise
support
survey
take instructions
train/teach
travel
tutor

This is just a small sampler of skills you may possess. Add to this list according to your own experience and interests. In addition to this list, I suggest you order the Self-Directed Search Kit from Psychological Assessment Research (PAR). Call 1-800-331-TEST to order. For under $20, you can take your own interest test and grade it yourself. It's extremely accurate, fun, and interesting to take! Once you become aware of your interests, skills, and options, you must then decide on a financial plan to ensure your success.

Making a Career Change without Going Broke

One of the main reasons people stay in careers that are not satisfying to them is because they don't want to give up the financial lifestyle they've become accustomed to. Many individuals believe that in order to change careers, they have to give it all up and become a starving artist. This simply is not true. Yes, it seems ideal to have a life like John Grisham who left his law practice for a year and wrote his first novel; however, most of us aren't in a financial position to take a year off to pursue a new career.

Instead we must have a solid financial plan in place before making any major career changes. Priscilla Grant did just that. After deciding to leave her career as managing editor at *Glamour* magazine, Priscilla began the task of building a nest egg. She and her mate maximized the assets they had, made automatic deposits from her paycheck into a mutual fund, and cut back on dining and entertainment expenses.

Within a year they were able to move to an area they both loved, and Priscilla pursued a career in freelance writing, which has given her the peace of mind she had been missing. If she hadn't instituted a smart financial plan, Priscilla would not have been able to maintain a peaceful state of mind. Constant financial stress will negate pursuing another career to achieve a fulfilling peace of mind.

Bridging the Gap to a New Career

As I stated earlier in the book, in order for me to make the transition to writing and counseling as a full-time career, I had to cover my expenses and gain the necessary experience in order to make it work well. It took me approximately one and a half years to accomplish this goal. Once you've decided on what career you would like to pursue, developed a financial plan to get you there, and determined what skills are necessary to your chosen profession, it's time to put the plan into action.

For example, if you have decided to become an interior designer, besides taking the necessary classes, you can offer your services to friends and family for barter or a reduced cost. (Remember, you are in training, so although you don't want to charge top dollar, charging nothing will devalue you and your services.) Use this opportunity to develop confidence in your abilities and gain word-of-mouth referrals.

In addition to moonlighting, you can also volunteer your time to organizations. Using the interior design example, I suggest you can offer your services to your community center in exchange for their showcasing your talents and your company sign. Offer your services in conjunction with another business owner and collaborate. I teamed up with a resume company that desired resume clients. I offered them the names of clients whom I was counseling, in exchange for their referring to me people who were interested in career counseling.

Even if you aren't going into business for yourself, you still have many options for bridging the career gap.

How to Convince Employers to Take a Chance on You

Take Peter for example. Peter was an aerospace software engineer who decided to pursue the new-home construction field. After assessing his transferable skills, he was convinced he had the necessary qualifications to locate a project management career in the construction industry.

He started his research by conducting informational interviews with several of the builders in the Dallas area. (Peter did not call those companies he desired to get employment with.) He interviewed many of the key decision makers and uncovered the most important and enticing qualities these individuals looked for when hiring.

Peter went to work. He developed a presentation that not only met but exceeded the expectations of the top three builders in his community. Peter wrote a creative and compelling cover letter that landed him interviews with all three firms. What Peter offered them was something no one else in the industry had: a tremendous knowledge of software development; he had spent his nights and weekends devising a way this software could improve company profits.

Peter's biggest dilemma was choosing between the two job offers he received. The last we spoke, Peter had been promoted and was well on his way in his new career. He did take a small salary cut in order to change careers; however, he was able to negotiate an increase after six months and is now making 25% more than he was in the aerospace industry.

FIVE TIPS FOR GETTING YOUR FOOT IN THE DOOR TO A WHOLE NEW INDUSTRY AND CAREER

1. Do your research. Conduct information interviews and learn from hiring officials before you take the plunge.
2. Develop a creative approach to getting noticed (send compelling cover letters, request introductions from networking contacts, avoid using only classified ads).
3. Go the extra mile. Discover what you offer that others don't and market this quality.

4. Volunteer your services.
5. Don't take NO for an answer.

Looking for a new career while currently employed is like working two full-time jobs. If you have the resources or can cut back on your expenses and work a part-time or temporary job during the transition, you can often speed up the process. However, you must be the judge of what works best for you. Spending valuable time to keep away the bill collectors won't speed up the process at all.

Great Interviewing Ideas to Help the Employers Forget You Aren't in Their Industry

Carrie was in sports marketing for five years when she decided to pursue a career in public relations for the hospitality industry. Having no previous background in either area, Carrie read all the most up-to-date trade journals for both industries. She gathered from the tone of the articles and her informational interviews that the industry lingo was a bit different from what she was accustomed to. After gearing her resume to reflect her transferable skills and volunteer experience that related to this industry, she received several interviews.

Carrie faced some tough competition. Every person she was up against for any job opening had prior experience in the hotel industry. What Carrie brought to the table was pure enthusiasm and hunger, which the others lacked. During the course of these interviews, Carrie used the industry lingo but took it a step further. She was careful not to use a buzzword just to impress others. Carrie made sure that when she talked the industry language, she knew what it meant and could frame it in a way to put the employer's mind at ease. Not only did Carrie end up getting an offer, but her future employer told her that although the other applicants had much more experience, her enthusiasm and obvious dedication to being prepared got her the job.

FIVE TIPS TO CLINCH AN OFFER

1. Learn the industry lingo to put an employer's mind at ease.
2. Be open and nondefensive about not having industry experience and use concrete examples of how your transferable skills and ability to learn quickly have resulted in a proven track record of success.

3. Explain how your nonindustry experience can be helpful to them (you don't have the bad habits found in the industry; you're open-minded; you can be easily trained in "their way").
4. Offer a guarantee. (Tell them you'll work a whole week for one dollar, and if they aren't thrilled at the end of the week, you'll part ways; if they are happy with the results, and we know they will be, they must offer you an opportunity for a paid position.)
5. Put your heart and soul into it. Show your enthusiasm (not desperation).

Over the years I've counseled individuals who have changed from engineer to high school algebra teacher, park district counselor to district manager in corporate America, accountant to interior designer, and on and on goes the list. Your career change doesn't have to be drastic; it can be more subtle—it all lies in what is best for you. No one knows better than you what career suits you best. No test in the world can tell you more than you know yourself. The key here is to ask yourself the right questions often enough to get the answers that are right for you. Use your inner-knowingness, your intuition, and your heart, and you won't make a mistake. Yes, you'll have doubts and fears along the way—that's part of the risk and part of the price of discovering success. Once you've entered a new career, you'll not only get some terrific payoffs, but you'll feel passion again for yourself and your life. My own career change is proof of that, and you can have "it," too.

Checklist for Moving On

	Yes	No
1. Did you make a list of your feelings regarding your current position?	___	___
2. Have you taken the necessary actions to resolve your current situation?	___	___
3. Have you taken the steps to determine your interests and desires?	___	___
4. Did you identify your skills on the transferable skills list?	___	___
5. Have you taken the time to outline a solid financial plan?	___	___

(continued)

Checklist (*continued*)

		Yes	No
6.	Have you taken steps to "bridge the gap" between careers?	___	___
7.	Have you taken the time to research the industries you wish to pursue?	___	___
8.	Are you prepared to interview effectively?	___	___
9.	Have you followed your heart and faced your fears regarding a career change?	___	___

► *13* ◄

Turning Trends into Jobs

What to Read, What to Watch, What to Do

When I look into the future, it's so bright it burns my eyes.
Oprah Winfrey

After writing *Getting Hired in the '90s*, I found myself a frequent interview subject and public speaker. During my many years as a recruiter and career counselor, I observed trends in hiring—taking note of what industries were on the verge of booming and noticing what skills seemed to make an impression on hiring authorities. This helped me give good advice to my clients. Of course, all this also helped me to develop a sort of sixth sense—call it intuition—for spotting trends before they really became big. I attributed this ability to pretty uncanny gut instincts. People in the media referred to me as a "futurist."

It's hard not to think about the future. How we act in almost every stage of our lives reflects how we think about the future. Some people are fearful of the future, of not knowing what the next day will bring. Other people have a basic optimism that keeps them in a positive mind-set about the very same state of uncertainty.

It is possible to lose the *fretful-about-the-future blues*. The first step is to become *your own futurist*, and *everyone can*. As soon as you make a commitment to notice things in your life, your community, and the world around you, you too can spot trends that will be of use to you. What does your intuition tell you about the things you see now? Do you ever get gut feelings about what you could do with the information you pick up every day? Prices at the store, new businesses you see at the local strip mall, things you read in the newspaper—what is your world of today telling you about your world of tomorrow? Based on information or trends you see now, you can plan your next series of career moves. How can you take the right steps now to make your future exciting and rewarding? Let's take a look at what's happening in the world.

You Are Your Own Best Gauge of Consumer Trends

Faith Popcorn, a popular marketing guru (and another promoted "futurist"), has based her consulting practice on spotting consumer trends. In one of her national bestsellers, *The Popcorn Report*, she described the biggest consumer trend of the '90s (a more full-blown version of a trend that started in the late '70s): "cocooning." Cocooning is about people trying to spend as much time as possible in the safety and comfort of their home. Working, entertaining, pursuing hobbies—more and more activities are reflecting the high value being placed on home life. First, let's look at some likely growth industries based on this trend. Then let's look at what kinds of jobs these industries require.

Expected growth industries	Job implications
Carry out/delivery services	Any type of business or job involved in bringing products or services directly to a consumer's home
Home entertainment, security, and consumer electronics	Any job involved in marketing to consumers at home (such as computer programming/database management, graphic art for direct mail projects, list brokers, and so on)
Casual clothing	
Do-it-yourself industry (suppliers and publications)	
Home health remedies	Engineering and product management in consumer electronics
	Sales and service of products/services for home entertainment or security
	Careers in development or marketing of home health products such as self-diagnostic kits, aroma therapy, and so on.

What do you think about jobs that might be related to this co-cooning trend? These are just a few examples of industries many of us are already seeing as growing. Take a few minutes to think about other consumer trends you've noticed. What's hot now? Do you think these are fads or do they say something bigger about what people de-sire? *Can you see yourself in an industry supporting a certain trend?*

Sometimes the best way to start thinking about how consumer trends might turn into a new career is to consider your own experi-ence as a consumer. Chris Fink was a marketing executive based out of Chicago for a manufacturer of disposable trays. She traveled about 70% of the time and always felt under some sort of pressure. Three years ago, after diagnosing herself as one of the stressed-out masses, she began going to a spa. There she got hooked on massage therapy. It improved her physical and emotional well-being so much that she started to barter bookkeeping for bodywork. Having a business/mar-keting orientation from the get-go, she found herself unable to stop thinking about the business side of this service. As getting her regular massage became more and more important to her, she started to think of ways to get more people like her—stressed-out corporate war-riors—to enjoy the same benefits.

On a part-time basis at first, she went into partnership with her masseuse, Wyman Hall-Walker. Their initial focus was on making their services accessible and affordable for people who needed it. Their company, Hired Hands, provides on-site therapeutic massage. Generally they work with companies to arrange "massage days," scheduled days when individual employees can sign up for affordable 15- to 20-minute chair massage sessions. Since the service has proved to boost productivity, some client companies started programs for giv-ing sessions as incentives (such as rewards for meeting quarterly quo-tas), and other companies are even starting to offer short massage ses-sions as standard company benefits.

Chris used her own experience as a consumer and listened to her intuition. She's now developing an exciting new career that still less than two years old, continues to develop and change. And Chris has discovered a new way of doing business—through partnerships.

Every time you develop business through partnerships, it tends to give you a new perspective on other things you can do. If my insight serves me well, this way of doing business is sure to be a trend into the millennium. Chris and her partner, Wyman, now have 15 therapists performing on-site massage for their corporate and individual clients. Through new alliances, they have also found themselves drawn in new directions. Working with nutritional counselors and companies that do blood pressure testing, they have started taking part in company-sponsored health fairs. Instead of competing with health spas, gym-based practitioners, or hands-on healers advertised in New Age magazines, they've started to do work *with* companies serving trade shows, and now have several major contracts providing chair massages in exhibition booths. Once Chris combined her personal experience with a bigger consumer trend, in her own words, "Doors have opened in other areas which I could not have anticipated."

Déjà-Vu All Over Again: Learning from the Lessons of History

Sometimes people become aware of trends because they notice their own changing habits as a consumer. Sometimes, when people have a lot of experience in a particular industry, they notice when things are being done like they were at some other time in history. Then they try to examine the opportunities that the first wave generated.

Neil Cacciottolo is in the music business—a lot of people might consider that an oxymoron. Many people who are into music don't tend to operate very well as businesspeople. There are a lot of dreamers. But Neil, who runs production and promotion services out of Nashville and Chicago, has succeeded by following some basic principles and using some lessons from history:

1. *Watch current industry behaviors and relate them to past industry trends.* Neil observed that most record labels don't put in much time or effort promoting a large number of their artists. They focus on only a handful expected to be moneymakers. In the early '60s, there were a lot of small labels that succeeded by getting airplay for new artists who needed to be developed and promoted. That is, they succeeded by devoting time and attention to their clients' careers. A lot of us might remember the movies about Buddy Holly or Rudy Valance, the scenes where they tooled around the country so that they could get in the faces of important radio station program directors. Getting in

front of these people can still be done by independents with a system for promotion in place. Neil decided to use press packages and mailings instead of an old Chevy.

2. *Pick out role models in your field of interest and study what they did to be successful.* Neil confessed his admiration for Paul McCartney and Herb Alpert. He made it a point to notice how they integrated their art with their business. A key lesson from both of these industry icons was to stay in control of producing your product and financing your business. Work in small steps, if necessary, to keep control. Neil set up his own studio and took out only small loans for very specific purposes (like new equipment) when he could pay them back quickly. Each aspect of his current operation was added slowly and only when all the required pieces were in place.

3. *Diversify your skills.* Get the necessary credentials. In Chapter 7, we talked about lifelong learning and the importance of getting the right credentials to do certain jobs. These credentials could be educational degrees, but they can also be licenses or affiliations. Neil had nine years of musical training and the appropriate educational credentials, but he didn't stop there. He made it a point to apprentice as a sound engineer with Chess Records to pick up credentials for the production side of his business. He also chose to affiliate himself with ASCAP so that he could have publishing rights to songs he or his artists produced. After many years in which popular wisdom suggested specialization, there has been almost a retreat to past times, and diversity of experience within an industry has become more of an asset again.

4. *Think of the power of diversity and synergy.* Neil's company now has seven divisions. He promotes artists and manages studio production, manufactures media, publishes songs, and consults for artists and independent labels. Each aspect of his business offers pathways for building on new parts. This seems to be a popular theme in developing new businesses or new job opportunities: **Take traditional, in-demand services, and combine them in new ways.** How can you combine your skills or industry experience in a new way?

5. *Think globally.* One of the biggest keys to Neil's success is his foresight in thinking globally. In Neil's case, a large portion of his business involves marketing blues, Christian, and gospel music in international markets. He's taken what he knows well—promotion of artists to radio stations and booking agents—and has applied his systems to new markets.

The People Principle

Consumer trends tend to point to which industries are going to become big or bigger. In many ways, predicting consumer trends is only a half step away from identifying job trends—if people choose to buy something, other people will have to make it, sell it, and serve it up the way consumers want it. There are other ways to evaluate job trends, though. One way is to notice changing demographics.

In the early '90s, I began to notice a shift in the recruiting industry. More and more job candidates requested my advice on interviewing skills and fewer employers requested advice on hiring new employees. I sensed this change was here for the duration. I realized the marketplace was changing and so must I. I was used to charging my client companies a fee; now I charged the job-seeker instead. It was difficult, at first, to charge for advice I once gave away for free.

Change of any type usually comes with a little discomfort, but it also opens up new opportunities. This is really true if you're trying to spot job trends and put yourself in position to build a career in a new area. Read census reports or demographic surveys. Consider demographic trends such as how the population is aging, the concentration of baby boomers in a given market, grown children living with parents, and so forth.

What do these trends tell you about new job opportunities? I believe the demand for home health care services that would help working people take care of aging parents is going to grow. This kind of information, combined with bigger consumer trends, might stir up all sorts of ideas. Try a few ideas on for size. See how they feel. Envision yourself operating in a certain kind of marketplace. Think of how these trends might require new products or skills or services. Once you have some ideas on growth industries that are interesting to you, research how you might acquire the skills you need to put yourself where you desire to be a few years from now.

After getting additional training in career counseling, I offered my services to groups (pro bono) to gain the experience and credibility necessary to enhance my future. As my knowledge and experience grew, so did my fees. I specifically created and executed my plan to become a national career and employment expert. Now, five years later, I give workshops and conduct speeches around the country, and the demand is on-going. I reformulate this plan every six months to keep up with the trends and plan out my next year. This review of feedback and trends has led to my conducting corporate workshops on team building in order to meet the growing need in the marketplace.

Watching changing legislation is another way to predict job trends before a market is glutted. The Americans with Disabilities Act (ADA) stirred up a lot of reevaluation of how buildings and public facilities were built and maintained. ADA consciousness also caused many companies to rethink how handicapped individuals operated in different work environments. Many new businesses sprouted up to help disabled individuals in the workplace. A lot of "green legislation"—laws protecting the environment—has had a similar impact. As recycled products and safe waste disposal systems continue to gain popularity, there will be a greater demand for people who can perform the varied functions within these industries.

Taking Your Pulse as a Futurist

Let's take a minute to take your pulse as a "career-focused" futurist:

▶ Do you read magazines, newsletters, or reports that cover major breakthroughs or changes in your industry?

▶ Do you know a little about your industry's past—its history before it became your career? Do you know about companies besides your own?

▶ Do you read or seek out information that showcases consumer trends and interests outside of your industry?

▶ Do you read your community paper or keep in touch with people in your network to pick up other types of information?

▶ Do you ever link information from one source with information from another source? Have you ever cut out a news article from a local paper and noted how it fit in with something you saw on a television program like *Dateline NBC?*

▶ Are you aware of your own changing habits as a consumer?

▶ Do you ever think about how your skills or background might be applied in different areas?

▶ Are you able to visualize career possibilities, try them on, and get in touch with your intuition by asking yourself clear-cut questions (see Chapter 3: "Discovering Your Special Purpose") to see if these possibilities *feel right?*

Moving from a trend spotter to someone who's prepared to move forward takes initiative. Sometimes, it takes other perspectives, too. A great way to be proactive instead of just conscious involves setting up an advisory board. In Chapter 8, we talked about developing a personal "sales force" to benefit from not only other people's ability to bring you into new circles but also the credibility that their referrals can give you. When you develop an advisory board, information flows the other way, from their world views to yours. Advisory board members are people you can count on to give you useful information that you might not normally come across.

You'll want to plan to talk to people on your advisory board regularly, though you may never meet formally. You can include some people from your own industry and other people from different backgrounds and disciplines as well. Comparing perspectives on trends is a great way to clarify your own thinking. Using advisory board members as a sounding board for your ideas on how to combine your skills with things happening in your world is also a good first step in developing an action plan. The ideal career you might create for your future self may require several small steps now that other people can help you plan.

Making the Most of the BIG Picture

When we discussed lifelong learning (Chapter 7), we pointed out how some skills are very specific to certain careers and other skills are transferable. The same might be true about mind-sets for developing rewarding careers. Some perspectives really apply to a lot of different industries. Two things in particular might help everyone envision new opportunities for themselves:

1. The world has become overstocked with information. Careers that involve helping people manage and use information seem sure to be on the rise.
2. The world is getting bigger and smaller at the same time. Rather, our awareness of other people and places is getting bigger while obstacles for communicating and doing business globally are getting smaller.

The software industry has always been one in which a company's success or failure depends on how well it can predict and ride a trend. Mark Fabish's company, Insight Software, markets a "process improvement" software product. Instead of creating ways to store more data, this software is used to help individuals or companies analyze information and make decisions. The growth of consulting businesses, home-office organizers, and specialized management companies bears the need for this type of product or service. Life seems to be getting complex. Careers involving helping people make decisions are going to continue to grow.

The "small world" concept is not new. Between the stories we hear about the Internet, and reading labels on the products we buy, it's easy to see that the world is our supermarket. What many people don't always think about is that the **world can also be our job market.** This has a lot of implications.

More trade opportunities means more opportunities to apply what you know in other places. (Think about Neil Cacciottolo marketing the blues in France.) More trade opportunities also means a deep and thorough understanding of foreign industries will be tremendously valuable to American companies doing business globally. I could relay countless stories about individuals who have great careers with large corporations because they understood silver mining in Mexico or silk production in Sri Lanka. The opening up of former communist countries, too, and efforts to "privatize" industries has created a huge demand for people with international finance skills, language skills, and a knowledge of foreign regulations. When you envision yourself in the career of your dreams, don't stop yourself from imagining the Taj Mahal, the docks in Athens, or the Danube River in the background, because some consumer or some business nearby just might need exactly what you can offer.

Checklist for Moving On

	Yes	No
1. Do you read more than one publication each month that features different perspectives on your industry or on changes in the world?	___	___
2. Can you identify two or three consumer trends that are particularly interesting to you?	___	___
3. How might your skills or interests relate to different industries? Can you think of two different ways to apply what you know to perform jobs in these new markets?	___	___
4. Pick two different work situations. Can you envision yourself in these new spaces? What does your gut seem to tell you about each one?	___	___
5. Can you think of four or five people whom you would like on your advisory board?	___	___
6. Do you have a global perspective on job opportunities?	___	___

▶ *14* ◀

Balancing It All!

**I don't know the key to success, but the key to failure
is trying to please everybody.**
Bill Cosby

One of the primary motivations I had when changing my career and
lifestyle was to create a more balanced and peaceful life for myself and
my children. Without balance—whether too much fun, relaxation,
or too much work, when the scales tip too far to one side—we get
"out of whack" and are good to no one, including ourselves.

Balance requires thought, planning, and action. In the book *First
Things First* (New York: Simon & Schuster, 1994), Stephen Covey
talks about balancing the four needs all humans have: *physical, social,
mental, and spiritual.* He explains that all four needs affect one other.
"When we aren't feeling well, it's much harder to think clearly, to relate in positive ways to others, to focus on contribution instead of survival. Only when we see the interrelatedness and the powerful synergy of these four needs do we become empowered to fulfill them in a
way that creates true inner balance, deep human fulfillment, and joy."

Are You Living in Balance?

I have the pleasure of meeting with thousands of individuals throughout the year, both in my consulting and speaking practice. A question
I often ask of them is either, "What do you enjoy doing?" or "What
hobby or interest are you involved in?" More often than not the response I get is, "Oh, I don't know . . ." or "I used to like such and
such." Then I will ask, "When was the last time you did something

191

just for you, or participated in this hobby?" Again, the response is typically, "Well, it's been a while" or "Gee, I can't remember." This is sad to me. And to them. However, it's never too late to change that aspect of your life.

Make a list of all the activities you enjoy or have interest in learning about. Ask yourself when was the last time you participated in something because YOU wanted to—not because you were supposed to or because your spouse or friend wanted you to. Now prioritize this list. Of all the activities or interests that appeal to you the most, are any of these activities something you can fit into your budget? (Perhaps you love to ski and haven't gone in several years, but the cost is a bit prohibitive right now—you can always plan for a trip somewhere down the line, or attend a local ski-show and just enjoy being around other skiers or visualizing your trip.)

Daily Balance

Once you've made your list and prioritized your interests, you'll want to plan for them. Just like we plan our daily activities, we must also schedule time for ourselves. I suggest planning personal time at least once a day. It doesn't have to be for a long period of time—even 10 minutes for meditating or taking a short walk is valuable. If you don't have some time for yourself each and every day, you are not in balance.

As a single working mother, I used to put the needs of my children, friends, and clients before my own. I found myself becoming resentful and stressed out. Now, each day, I take time for me. Whether it's a warm and relaxing bath, private reading time, a walk, listening to my favorite music, or playing tennis, I do it! Without fail. I have become very attached to "my time" and seldom let anything interrupt it. I have found that I don't often become stressed out like I used to. And I'm teaching my girls an important lesson: Take care of yourself. When you feel good about you, you can be there for others. If you aren't there for yourself, you cannot—no matter how much you want to—be there for others!

Now if you are tempted to say, "I just don't have any more time in the day left for me. I would like to have more time to balance, but with work, kids, spouse, and other family—well, I need an extra two hours per day." Will you have the time when you have a heart attack? Will you have the time when you are retired? Will you have the time when you are so sick you can't get out of bed? Make the time now, or you may never see it again.

I learned a lesson as a young girl from my grandfather. For 25 years he was a postman in the Chicago area. He and my grandmother planned for years to retire early and move to the South to have fun. Two weeks before he retired, he succumbed to a heart attack and never got the chance. He was such a wonderful man, always doing for others . . . always thinking he'd have time to enjoy what he wanted . . . later on. Except later on never came. In his death he inspired me to live.

Balancing Family

Although I am not married any longer, I do have an active social life, and making time for family and children can be a challenge! When my girls were younger, I recall feeling as though I had all the time in the world with them. How wrong I was! I can remember being anxious for my oldest daughter to learn to crawl, then to walk and talk, and to start school. Now that she's a teenager, I wonder what my hurry was! Balancing family starts with "living in the moment," enjoying the time we have now.

If you have children or family, I encourage you to examine how much quality time you spend with them. And if you do spend the time, are you really all there, or are you just there physically but somewhere else mentally? Practice spending time with them and focusing on the here and now. Remind yourself often that we only have today—no one knows if we have tomorrow.

Plan things together that will meet the whole family's needs. For example, I am planning to take a family trip after I finish this book. I want some relaxation time for myself, but I also want to share my time off with my children. They want to go somewhere fun and exciting. We pooled all our interests and decided on a cruise to the Caribbean that includes a visit to Disney World. This is a win-win trip for all! I can relax and enjoy adult entertainment while they swim, enjoy planned activities, and go to their favorite theme park— all in one trip. Look for ways to negotiate with your family so that all or at least some of everyone's needs are met.

Tell the people you care about you love them each and every day! Give and get at least three or more hugs per day! Hugs are great for stress reduction and will help you and others to keep balanced.

Balancing a Career with a Personal Life

In today's busy world, it isn't abnormal to put in 50 hours plus per week into work (with travel time and overtime expected). For anyone who owns a business (especially one run from home), it takes extra effort to balance work and personal time. I've found a couple of solutions that may make your life a bit easier.

Write down all your daily and weekly responsibilities, chores, and obligations. Make a list of those tasks you don't enjoy all that much and can delegate or hire out. For example, I would rather do almost anything than grocery shop. Not only does it require a couple of hours each week, but I just don't enjoy it very much. So to solve this problem, I've engaged a computerized grocery shopping service that delivers my groceries weekly. For a small monthly fee and delivery cost, I have eliminated this source of frustration from my weekly schedule. I have also found that this service actually ends up saving me money as well as time. I used to impulsively buy items that were not on my list when I would visit the store. Now I stick to the computerized list and have discovered that my monthly grocery bills are far less than they used to be!

I've done the same with running errands and cleaning. Anything you don't like to do that you can hire out—I encourage you to do so. Use the time you save from these tasks to create more business opportunities or to get involved in activities you enjoy. Even when I was on a very limited budget (in other words when I was nearly broke!), I was able to barter my services (consulting) with a cleaning service in the area. This saved me several hours per week and freed me up to spend the weekends with my kids.

Look for ways at work to use more effective time management skills, so that you eliminate as much overtime as possible from your workweek. You may want to utilize the services of a time management or business coach to assist you in doing that.

Balancing Your Physical, Mental, Spiritual, and Social Needs

Physical Needs

Remember the good old days when in the midst of our daily learning we got to go outside for recess? How great it felt to breathe fresh air and to play? I long for those days when in the middle of everything I could get out and rejuvenate myself. When I was a recruiter, I spent much of my day in a high-rise office building with no windows that opened and no fresh air to breathe. I often ate lunch at my desk and many times arrived at work in the dark and left in the dark. What a life!

I spent my weekends catching up on all the sleep I missed and seldom got physical exercise of any kind. People used to tell me how important exercise was to me, and I just listened and smiled. Yes, I knew that, but I hated exercise. So I didn't do any. What I have since discovered is that exercise can be something to enjoy. I do not enjoy working out in a health club, although I know many people who do; instead, I like swimming and tennis and bicycle riding. I now balance my day and week with a little of each. I must admit, though, when I find myself deluged with work, I literally have to force myself to keep these activities in my schedule. When I am tempted to let them go for awhile, I remind myself of how wonderful I feel when I am active, and this helps me to keep the balance in my physical life.

When I feel emotionally healthy, I find myself physically healthy. So now when I become run-down or feel ill, I immediately stop to ask myself what is going on. I literally ask myself what my body or mind needs in order to reenergize itself. By checking in with myself on a daily basis, I've found that my health stays balanced and I'm feeling better now than I did in my 20s.

Besides exercise, preventive health care requires knowing yourself. I am a big advocate of massage therapy and include it in my weekly activities. I also look for alternative, holistic ways of keeping my physical well-being in tact. I listen to soothing music, meditative tapes, eat a healthy diet, and so on.

When I do succumb to illness, I really take the time to recover. I used to go to work even when I was sick. Not only would I spread whatever I had to everyone else, I often got worse. In fact, I once had a cold that I left untreated and attempted to work through. Rather than resting and allowing myself to heal, I forged ahead. I ended up in the hospital with pneumonia and was off almost an entire month. Oh, an ounce of prevention! Your body will tell you loud and clear when you need healing—learn to listen to it! I suggest reading Louise Hay's *You Can Heal Your Life* (Curlsbard, CA: Hay House, 1996)—it works wonders.

Mental Needs

We have already covered this subject throughout this book. Much of a successful attitude and healthy balance is generated through our mental abilities. Reread Chapters 1 through 3 for a complete run-down on mental balance. In addition, for great direction and a wealth of information on mental power and balance, read *Awaken the Giant Within* (New York: Simon & Schuster, 1992) and listen to the Personal Power Tapes (Irwindale, CA: Gothy Renken Corporation, 1989), both by Anthony Robbins. For those interested in workshops or seminars relating to personal growth, I heartily recommend a course called "Understanding Yourself and Others" put on by The Global Relationship Centers, Inc., out of Austin, Texas.

Spiritual Needs

This subject is covered extensively in Chapter 10, and I encourage you to add to your spiritual balance by reading and getting more in touch with this part of yourself. The following are some great books to get you started:

Return to Love, Marianne Williamson (New York: Harper, 1992).
Seven Spiritual Laws of Success, Deepak Chopra (San Rafael, CA: New World Library, 1994).
The Seat of the Soul, Gany Zukav (New York: Simon & Schuster, 1990).
The Prophet, Kahil Gibran (New York: Knopf, 1952).
The Teachings of the Masters of the Far East, B. Spaulding (Marina del Ray, CA: DeVorss Publications, 1992).
Autobiography of a Yogi, Paramahansa Yogananda (Los Angeles: Self-Realization Fellowship, 1994).

Social Needs

In this busy world of ours, we often avoid making and developing new friendships because of lack of time. Friendships are extremely impor-tant to having social balance. If you haven't made a new friend in the past six months, I suggest you take the time and effort to do so. Peo-ple come and go in our lives, and as we grow older, it takes a commit-ment to link up with others. When we were children, making new friendships was a priority in our lives. As adults we forget how benefi-cial friends can be. Many adults are very lonely and have difficulty making new friends. Reread Chapter 8 on building relationships and take action to develop social acquaintances.

Plan some "play time." As I've said throughout this book, we adults can learn a lot from children. Play is vital to having a balanced life. Life can be filled with fun if you allow it. Remember, though, life is a balance of joy and sorrow. They are intermingled and inseparable. Many joyful things can come from sorrow and pain if you look for them. At the beginning of this book, I asked you to write your definition of success. Take a moment now and write it again. Is it the same? Different? Ask yourself what you've learned about life and yourself.

Because life is eternal, there really is no end to the teachings of this book and life—just a continuation of learning. We can embrace life's teachings and live a fulfilled journey, or we can fight them. I hope by sharing my life lessons and those of others with you, I have encouraged you to choose a fulfilled life, one of purpose, power, and prosperity into and beyond the year 2000. Peace to all.

Checklist for Moving On

	Yes	No
1. Did you make a list of the activities you enjoy?	___	___
2. Have you planned at least one new activity and taken action on it?	___	___
3. Have you spent quality time with your family recently?	___	___
4. Did you make a list of tasks that you can delegate or hire out?	___	___
5. Have you planned and taken action on physical activity?	___	___
6. Have you spent time reviewing your emotional health and taking action on enhancing it?	___	___
7. Have you participated in or read some spiritual guidance?	___	___
8. Did you take action on meeting a new friend or playing more?	___	___

About the Author

Vicki Spina's knowledge of career trends and success methods stems from her 18-year successful track record in the employment and consulting industry. Vicki is an award-winning recruiter and the author of *Getting Hired in the '90s* (Chicago: Dearborn Publishers, 1995).

Ms. Spina owns Corporate Image, a consulting service in the suburbs of Chicago that specializes in career and employment issues. She has appeared on more than 100 radio programs, as a career strategist for CNBC, and was featured twice on NBC's popular morning program *TODAY*. Several excerpts from her book as well as articles she has written on employment issues are currently being published in leading magazines.

In addition to her consulting practice, Vicki is also a sought-after national speaker and conducts workshops based on the principles of *Success 2000*.

For information regarding Ms. Spina's services, seminars, or speaking engagements, please write or call:

Michelle Rathman c/o
Impact! Communications, Inc.
21 Vernon Ct. Ste. 100
South Elgin, IL 60177
(847) 608-9177

Vicki celebrates her life and journey with her daughters Carli, age 14, and Caitlyn, age 10, in the suburbs of Chicago. Ms. Spina also volunteers her time to Global Relationship seminars (an organization dedicated to world peace), and she is actively involved at the community level to improve unemployment.

Index